muslimsnext door

muslimsnext door

UNCOVERING MYTHS AND CREATING FRIENDSHIPS

SHIRIN TABER

GRAND RAPIDS, MICHIGAN 49530 USA

Muslims Next Door
Copyright © 2004 by Shirin Taber

Requests for information should be addressed to:

Zondervan, *Grand Rapids, Michigan 49530*

Library of Congress Cataloging-in-Publication Data

Taber, Shirin, 1966–
    Muslims next door : uncovering myths and creating friendships / Shirin Taber
      p. cm.
    Includes bibliographical references.
    ISBN 0-310-25564-3
    1. Missions to Muslims—United States. 2. Islam. I. Title.
BV2625.T33 2004
261.2'6'0973—dc22

                                  2004008351

The website addresses recommended throughout this book are offered as a resource to you. These websites are not intended in any way to be or imply an endorsement on the part of Zondervan, nor do we vouch for their content for the life of this book.

Interior design by Sharon VanLoozenoord

Printed in the United States of America

04 05 06 07 08 09 10 /❖ DC/ 10 9 8 7 6 5 4 3 2 1

To Patricia Ann Madani and Pamela Ann McPoland
for their Christlike devotion to family and neighbors

CONTENTS

ACKNOWLEDGMENTS

I am deeply grateful to my editor, Paul Engle, and the staff of Zondervan, who believed in the power of my story. Thank you for mentoring me and making my dream to be a writer a reality. I'm also thankful to family members and friends with Muslim backgrounds who have opened my eyes to the virtues of honor, stylish modesty, hospitality, and the pursuit of beauty and excellence, and were the inspiration for this book.

Many thanks to those who encouraged me as a new author and spent hours reading my manuscript: my loving and patient husband, Clyde; my resilient children, Quinn, Elena, and Sage; my father; my brothers, Thom and Cameron; my relatives Emilie, Elaine, Michele, and Diane; and dear friends Pam and Dennis McPoland, Barbara and Roger MacDonald, Marsha, Kirsten, Alisa, Mary H., Robin, Anne, Larisa, Pebble, Mary P., Dan and Bridget, Jill and Janine, Peggy and Allan, Susan, Mary G., Donna, Dave E., Cy, David M., Jim L., Sky, Mark J., Chris S., Mike A., Lou Nelson, John Eames, Mark Rodgers, Paul Marshall, Dr. Miriam Adeney, Dr. Ralph Covell, and Pastor Lyle Castellaw.

Blessings, joy, peace (Matt. 5:16; 1 Peter 2:9). You have profoundly impacted my life and given me the courage to see myself as a writer.

Why I've Written This Book

Eileen, a stunning brunette in her thirties, caught my attention in the checkout line of an Albertson's store one crisp fall morning. I watched as she freely conversed with customers. I found myself drawn to her jewel-black eyes, olive coloring, and inviting smile, all of which reminded me of the many exotic women I had met over the years as I traveled in the Middle East: Mina from Iran, Leila from Tunisia, Hulya from Turkey. Eileen, however, is not of Middle Eastern origin, but Latino and, like me, is part of the browning of America.

A few months later, Eileen and I ran into one another at a Christmas tea hosted by my church. It intrigued Eileen to learn that I was to be the guest speaker that night. She thought of me as just a customer in the checkout line. Before the evening ended, she thanked me for my talk, which she said had touched her. Little did I know how profoundly.

The following week, Eileen pulled me aside at the checkout line and gave me a small gift. Inside a red box was a silver angel pendant. The gift, she said, was her way of expressing her gratitude for the things I had shared at the tea. My Middle Eastern background fascinated her, and she asked if we could get together sometime for coffee. She had a few questions, questions about Islam.

Over the years, various people who have been curious about Muslims have been brought into my path—parents of my childhood friends, a math teacher in junior high, businessmen at dinner parties, members of an adult Sunday school class, friends in my book club.

It took a few weeks to coordinate our schedules, but finally one afternoon Eileen made her way to my home. Eileen wondered if I could help her understand why Muslims are so angry with America. She has friends who are Muslims, and she wanted to learn about their point of view. After we were comfortably seated in my living room, I began to tell her about my background as a daughter of an Iranian-Muslim father and an Irish-Catholic mother. She heard for the first time an insider's view of Muslim life.

When the topic of 9-11 came up, she wondered about America's response. "Revenge? Strike back militarily? And how do we respond now to Muslims living in the United States?"

I turned the questions over in my mind, trying to think of the best way to respond. "Most Americans can't identify with the complex issues that fuel Muslims' mistrust toward the West and toward the American government in particular," I said. "We'd have to cover hundreds and hundreds of years of history to understand Muslim animosity. But regardless of how America responds to terrorism, there is an issue that is far more important, and one that each of us can do something about. We need to cultivate peace with Muslims living in our homeland. We need to make them feel a part of America. Make them feel like they belong. They aren't going to go away."

She nodded, trying to grasp the issues confronting our Muslim neighbors. I went on to explain that the Muslims shown on the news as gun-toting, flag-burning religious fanatics in some Middle Eastern country are not typical followers of Islam. The truth is that millions of North Americans and Europeans study with, work with, and live near Muslims. It's no longer uncommon to hear the names Fatima or Mohammed on campus, at a neighborhood park, or in a boardroom. In the past, Muslims have been marginalized in our homeland, seen as resident aliens and not as part of the fabric of our country. Christians in the West rarely have any close contact with practicing Muslims, leaving all discussions of religion and faith to missionaries overseas. But times have changed.

Our World After 9-11

When historians look back, it will be radical Islam and the war on terrorism that will mark our times. In our post–9-11 world, many Westerners are suspicious of their Muslim neighbors. Public anger against Muslims has increased. *Newsweek* reported a 1,700 percent rise in hate crimes against Arab-Americans since 9-11.[1] An ABC News poll showed that since the bombing of the Twin Towers and the Pentagon, and the downing of the plane in a field in Pennsylvania, Americans have an unfavorable view of Islam and think the Muslim faith encourages violence.[2] But many Americans, like Eileen, want to understand how Muslims think. Some want to know how to establish friendships that can point Muslims to Christ.

Times have changed, and Islam has become a presence in Western society. Since 1999, for example, Muslims have been conducting prayer inside the United States Capitol on Fridays. The number of Muslim chaplains in the United States military has tripled, serving 4,000 personnel.[3] In 2000, the United States Postal Service issued a postal stamp commemorating Ramadan, the ninth month of the Islamic year and the Muslim month of fasting. According to *Islamic Horizons,* an influential Muslim journal with more than 60,000 readers, "Muslim Americans represent $75 billion of collective income, more than any Muslim country can produce."[4]

Westerners are realizing that we can no longer be ignorant of the fastest-growing religion in the world. The number of Muslims worldwide is estimated to be over one billion, which is nearly one-sixth of the world's population.[5] United Nations statistics report that in Europe the Muslim population grew by more than 100 percent between the years of 1989 and 1998.[6] Nearly six million Muslims live in France, and three million in Germany, contributing to a total of fourteen million in all of Europe.[7] That's nearly four times as many Muslims as are in the United States.

The presence of nearly ten million Muslims in France and Germany helps shed light on why Europeans might see their relationship with the Middle East differently than do people in the United States. I often tell my friends in California, "Imagine how you'd feel if the world suddenly became hostile toward Mexico and the Mexicans who inhabit our communities, schools, and workplaces. The sentiment you'd feel, whether shock, sympathy, or fear, is comparable to how Europeans now feel toward the Muslims who have lived among them for centuries." Whether in Paris, Berlin, London, or Brussels, European Muslims are becoming a powerful political force, making world leaders understandably anxious to keep the peace and secure their votes.

Growth of the Muslim population is occurring not only in Europe. The percentage of Muslims in the United States is on the rise too, up 25 percent from 1989 to 1998. Why? Changes in immigration laws since 1960 and a demand for workers have encouraged Muslims to seek prosperity in our nation.[8] Estimates from *The Christian Science Monitor* put the current number of Muslims in this country at four million.[9] The number of mosques in North America is approaching 2,500.[10] A large number of Muslims populate our biggest cities, with principal concentrations found in Los Angeles, Chicago, and New York. There are 400,000 in the Chicago area, and another 400,000 residing in New Jersey.[11] Twenty percent of American Muslims live in California, and 16 percent in New York.[12] African-American converts make up nearly 45 percent of the Muslims in America.[13] Given this rapid growth, if there isn't already a Muslim living on your street or working near you or attending school with your children, there likely will be in the near future.

As an Iranian-American, I wonder how we might change our nation's perceptions of and ways of relating to the followers of Islam. I wonder if some of the answers to peaceful coexistence with Muslims lie in a change of heart and values by our nation's families and churches. I can't help but think of the powerful example of repentance and healing given to us by Pope John Paul II when he asked the Jews for forgiveness for the Holocaust and the Crusades.

Understanding the Issues

Learning to empathize with Muslims and to understand the issues that trouble them can help smother the flames of suspicion and the fear of terrorism. Too often when Muslims have caused violence against our country, Americans have blamed all Muslims, ignoring the fact that only a small minority acted violently against our nation. Some people have joined the ranks of talk-show hosts who berate Islam. Many believe everything negative they've ever heard about Muslims.

I've written this book out of deep respect for my Muslim family members and friends. My goal is to help readers in the West to better understand a Muslim perspective and to learn how to take steps to establish friendships which can point to Christ. I have avoided delving into Muslim-Christian theological differences, since other books already cover that ground in great detail; instead I have focused on points of commonality. My desire is to help facilitate understanding and mutual respect in our living and working situations and to help Westerners feel that Muslims are approachable. I want to encourage my readers to identify with their Muslim neighbors in a way that reveals the love and compassion of Christ.

Recalling the words of President George W. Bush, let us remember that "when we think of Islam, we think of a faith that brings comfort to millions of people, that's made up of brothers and sisters of every race. America counts millions of Muslims amongst our citizens, and Muslims make up an incredibly valuable contribution to our country. Muslims are doctors, lawyers, law professors, and members of the military, entrepreneurs, shopkeepers, moms and dads. And they need to be treated with respect. In our anger and emotion, our fellow Americans must treat each other with respect."[14]

In the pages that follow, you'll read the stories of people I know, like Ahmed and Leila, Hossein and Maryam. I'll take you into homes, universities, and offices in our nation's neighborhoods and cities where Westerners rub elbows with Muslims. My prayer is that by the time you reach the end of this book, you will have a better understanding of the Muslims in your sphere of relationships and you'll desire to befriend Muslims, enjoy the richness of their culture and values, and feel more equipped to point them to Christ in a gentle and respectful manner. As you read, ask God to open your heart and draw you closer to his love for Muslims. So turn the page and let's take a look inside the world of *Muslims Next Door*.

across the street and next door

Be kind to orphans,
and to the needy,
and to the neighbor who is kin,
and to the neighbor who is a stranger,
and to the companion at your side,
and to the traveler,
and to those whom your right hands own.

—THE KORAN, 4:36

Even though my mother was Catholic and had me baptized before my first birthday, I was born a Muslim because my father is a Muslim. He is from Iran, and I lived in Iran for five years as a child. Through a most unusual set of circumstances, I was exposed to a personal faith in Christ in my teen years. Let me tell you the story so you can catch a glimpse into the passion and emotion that drove my writing of this book.

The Story of Two Neighbors

It was 1979, just prior to the taking of fifty-two American hostages in Iran. Most afternoons, our neighbor Pamela walked across the street, knocked on the door of our home, and let herself in. With kids at school, Pamela and my mother were able to spend a peaceful hour or two before the demands of family life took over. Most days in Seattle, it drizzled and a light fog hovered above Lake Sammamish, which our home overlooked.

Over the years, Pamela had become accustomed to the unique furnishings in our home: Persian carpets, gold samovars, colorful ceramic and glass water pipes, and oriental artwork. When my father was home (once every three to four months from his work as an airline representative in Iran for Iran Air), the house smelled of saffron, cumin, dill, and mint. *Zereshk polo* or *ghormeh sabzee* gently cooked on the stove top. A kettle of water simmered contentedly throughout the day, ready for the preparation of hot tea—in our Middle Eastern home in the Northwest.

At times my mother, an American and a Catholic, felt overwhelmed by her multicultural marriage. Pamela was there to offer a listening ear and advice. It wasn't that Pamela's marriage was perfect, but she had a certainty about life which strengthened my mother and, most of all, gave her hope.

My father was due home again from Iran before Easter. Normally a time for rejoicing and happy reunions at Sea-Tac Airport, this time my mother felt unprepared for his visit. She worried that she might be losing him. She worried about her weight. They had been apart for two years because of my father's work for Iran Air. The separation had taken a toll on their marriage. Too much time apart had allowed his heart to wander.

As if in the fog that often gathered around the house, making familiar evergreens and the lake view disappear, my mother felt uncertain of the path ahead of her. She told Pamela of the years she had sacrificed her happiness to live in my father's country, enabling him to climb the corporate ladder. Because of his work, we lived in both Iran and the United States. A dozen times she had traversed the Atlantic Ocean with three small children, living like a nomad because of her commitment to her man. Now her sacrifices and her commitment seemed pointless. Divorce seemed imminent. How would she raise three children alone? What legal recourse would she have to collect child support as the spouse of a foreigner who lived five thousand miles away ten months out of the year? And as a Catholic, could she marry again?

Pamela listened and prayed for wisdom to help her friend. These were uncharted waters. She wondered where the answers were and how God could ever provide.

A Turning Point

The women continued to meet in the afternoons, plotting the revival of my parents' marriage. Together they went to Weight Watchers. They improved my mother's wardrobe, makeup, and, most important, her self-esteem. For a time, happy married life seemed in reach. But things took an unexpected turn when my mother became ill. She felt tired all the time. Eventually she found it hard to keep up with her secretarial work, and her employer asked her to leave her job. A few weeks later, she was so weak and tired that she had difficulty picking up us kids from school. Some mornings she could hardly get out of bed to pack our lunches. She became depressed and was terrified of what might be wrong. Her family doctor told her she was going through early menopause.

My mother became so weak that my father and I finally took her to an urgent-care facility. After blood tests, my mother was taken by ambulance to a hospital emergency room. Over the next days and weeks, blood transfusions and IVs, a respirator, emergency surgeries, and chemotherapy followed. Nothing helped. My mother died three months later from leukemia at the age of thirty-nine. I was fourteen.

My father was devastated. The loss seemed too great. He had just fled his country because of the Iranian Revolution of 1979, leaving a prestigious airline career. He worried about how he would care for his children. He was a man without a country, without a source of income. And now he had lost his wife.

Pamela quickly organized family and neighbors to make funeral arrangements and provide temporary child care for my brothers and me. She had often talked with my mother about the need to turn to Christ during a time of great need. Now she focused her efforts on my brothers and me. She cared for us, along with her own three children, with supernatural love. She fed us at her home, transported us to athletic events and on our paper routes, and, when our father returned to Iran to salvage his assets and look for a new wife, Pamela and her husband let us move in with them.

Back in Iran there would have been grandparents and uncles and aunts to stand in the gap for this Middle Eastern family, but in the

United States, with no relatives nearby, it took neighbors, teachers, coaches, and church volunteers to help raise three motherless Iranian-American children whose father was far away some of the time, in Iran. At times Pamela felt overwhelmed, nearly breaking down from exhaustion as she tried to raise six young adolescents. Never once did she allow cultural barriers and prejudices to stand in the way of God's calling to care for a family very different from her own. Lifted up by the prayers of other concerned families, she persisted and shared with us our need to know God personally, just as she had done with our mother. Through Pamela's influence, I, at the age of fifteen, began to take my faith more personally and started attending an evangelical church.

This story of my mother and Pamela—two women, two neighbors—has touched me deeply and served as my motivation for writing this book. I want to let others know how to approach Muslims in our country with the same grace and compassion that was shown to my family. I want to let others know how to help bring down the walls of suspicion and fear that inhibit us from demonstrating the love of Christ with our neighbors.

Who Is Your Neighbor?

Muslims are living among us. Countless Muslim families have immigrated to Western countries, including the United States. Perhaps you're curious about the personal life and beliefs of a Muslim colleague at your place of employment or a fellow student at your university and, while perusing the Islam section of titles in a bookstore, you picked up this book. You want to know more about Muslims, maybe even how to become friends with a Muslim family.

> It's no longer necessary to go to the Middle East as a tourist, a Peace Corps worker, or a missionary to learn about Muslim culture and the followers of Islam. God has brought them to the United States, enriching our nation with their talents and way of life.

The stories of the Muslims among us are all different. But the one constant for all is their desire to be accepted in this new country they've chosen. Muslims want to be included in the daily life of their neighborhoods, of their friends and coworkers. As Muslims navigate life's challenges in a culture that is not their own, opportunities abound for Christians to build bridges to their Muslim neighbors.

It's no longer necessary to go to the Middle East as a tourist, a Peace Corps worker, or a missionary to learn about Muslim culture and the followers of Islam. God has brought them to the United States, enriching our nation with their talents and way of life. In order to give you a glimpse into what life is like for Muslims in this country, let me give you some quick examples of the variety of Muslims I've met:

■ Ahmed and Leila live in Montréal with their three children. They moved to Canada from Jordan five years ago. Ahmed is worried that his wife has not learned to speak English properly. Leila has become melancholy, stuck at home with a toddler with asthma. She does not have a driver's license. Ahmed wishes his wife could develop a close friendship with one of the women in their apartment complex, but everyone seems so busy. Most of the women work outside the home.

■ Rashid is a struggling Lebanese student in Houston. Thanks to a relative, he was able to come to the United States to study two years ago. He goes to class during the day and works two jobs the rest of the week. He's homesick, misses an old girlfriend back home, and feels disconnected from American students on campus. He'd like to join a fraternity, but fears he'd be shunned. He second-guesses his decision to try to make a new life for himself in this country but fears there are no options for him back home.

■ Hulya, a Turkish woman, works as an accountant for a large firm in Los Angeles. She recently married, and her husband has asked her to wear a head scarf as a symbol of purity. She feels torn because of the rise in hostility toward Muslims in the United States since 9-11. She loves her husband but doesn't want to be ridiculed or make waves at work.

■ Two brothers, Ferhad and Murat, are among the fifteen thousand Iraqis in America whom the FBI interviewed as part of the

Homeland Security Department's Operation Liberty Shield. Like most Iraqi immigrants, they fled to this country to escape Saddam Hussein's brutal regime. Now they are terrified that they may be detained and possibly deported.

■ Maryam and Hossein are from Iran and are expecting their first child. Originally it was their plan to have Maryam's mother fly over from Iran for the birth and to help care for the baby. The mother now has heart problems and cannot make the long journey by plane. Maryam feels unprepared to care for the baby alone. In their culture, it is customary for grandparents and older women in the family to help young women make the transition to motherhood. She feels nervous about hiring a nanny and concerned about the expense of full-time child care.

A New Era of Fear and Suspicion

Since the horror of 9-11 and all the media coverage of anti-American protests, many Westerners look at Muslims, even ones like those I've mentioned above, with unease. In the back of some people's minds, maybe in your own mind, is mistrust of Muslims. In the past, Muslims hung on the fringes of society like dark shadows, but now the light of current events casts a glare of suspicion on them. Some may wonder, as they walk past a group of Muslim students on campus and see the length of the men's beards and the scarves worn by the women, whether the students are tied to terrorism or to some fundamentalist Muslim sect that is out to destroy this country.

> In the past, Muslims hung on the fringes of society like dark shadows, but now the light of current events casts a glare of suspicion on them.

Let me assure you that the majority of Muslims in America are like any typical American. They love the United States, and whether or not they become citizens, they want a chance to pursue their dreams and find happiness. They should not be judged by the actions of other Muslims. To do so would be the same as judging American Catholics and Protestants for the violence in Ireland, or to look suspiciously upon

Korean-Americans for weapons of mass destruction harbored in North Korea. We must resist any temptation to blame all Muslims residing among us for atrocities that originated outside our borders, sponsored by radical sects halfway around the world.

American poet and essayist Ralph Waldo Emerson wrote, "No people can be explained by their national religion. They do not feel responsible for it; it lies outside of them."[1] Emerson had the insight not to pass sweeping judgment on an entire group of people. To be American is to be Italian, Chinese, Irish, Japanese, Pakistani, Mexican, Greek, English, or dozens of other nationalities. Americans are Hindu, Buddhist, Catholic, Jewish, Protestant. Each of these world religions has something to be ashamed of in its past.

> To be American is to be Italian, Chinese, Irish, Japanese, Pakistani, Mexican, Greek, English, or dozens of other nationalities. Americans are Hindu, Buddhist, Catholic, Jewish, Protestant. Each of these world religions has something to be ashamed of in its past.

Muslims are living among us. We run into them at the laundromat, the post office, in taxis, and at doctors' offices. We rely on many of the services they provide. They are our doctors, architects, grocers, taxi drivers, and engineers. Our country is greater for all of their contributions. Our relationships are more diverse; our worldview has become broader.

I invite you to join me in the coming chapters in taking an honest look at some common myths about our Muslim neighbors so that we may overcome any barriers of suspicion and fear and live together in harmony—sit with one another in classes, live by each other in dorms, conduct business negotiations together, and as parents coordinate play groups, sporting events, and volunteer efforts at local schools. We'll look at misconceptions that many Christians have about Muslim spiritual beliefs.

As we examine these myths, it is my hope that you will begin to feel more comfortable to move toward Muslims in friendship and even be able to look for opportunities to share the heart of the gospel.

QUESTIONS FOR REFLECTION OR DISCUSSION

1. In the story of Pamela and my mother at the beginning of this chapter, what do you admire most about Pamela in her effort to reach out to her neighbor?

2. The chapter mentions several examples of Muslims living in North America. What examples can you add from your sphere of relationships? What are some of the needs of these people?

3. What might be some reasons why Christians are suspicious of Muslims?

4. Name some other people groups that have been mistrusted in the past. What can we learn from these other situations to help us now to relate to Muslims in our nation?

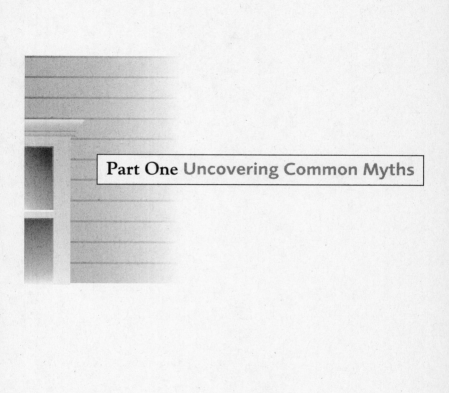

Part One Uncovering Common Myths

CHAPTER 2

Muslims and Christians have nothing in common spiritually

If you are a Christian, you do
not have to believe that all the
other religions are simply
wrong all through.

—C. S. LEWIS, *Mere Christianity*

"Shirin, it's been so long since we last spoke," Maryam, an Iranian friend, bemoaned. "I sent you pictures of my children at Christmas and left a message on your answering machine. Why have you lost touch?"

Ashamed, I listed my excuses, genuinely sorry to have disappointed my friend. "Life's been a whirlwind lately. Clyde's dad passed away last fall, the baby is into everything, and my brother is now living with us." Maryam and I had become friends at the University of Washington fifteen years earlier when we met in a Persian-language class.

She seemed reassured. "I'm sorry to hear it's been a hard year, but I'm glad you don't want to end our friendship. I worried that because of 9-11, you might not want to relate to your Muslim friends anymore."

I gasped, horrified that she would even think that. "No, I apologize!" I pleaded, knowing I had let her down. "If anything, I would've wanted my response to be the opposite. This is the time when I need to be your friend, not to draw away from you."

Maryam confirmed my suspicion that many Muslims living in the West now feel insecure about how to relate to non-Muslims. The slightest suggestion of rejection or animosity hurts them deeply.

> Maryam confirmed my suspicion that many Muslims living in the West now feel insecure about how to relate to non-Muslims. The slightest suggestion of rejection or animosity hurts them deeply.

Ostracized in Junior High

Maryam's fears reminded me of the pain I felt in junior high being ostracized during the Iranian Revolution. It was the winter of 1979 and Iran captured the attention of the world when the shah, Muhammad Reza, fled his country, presumably on vacation, and never returned. The government collapsed and the Ayatollah Khomeini, a Muslim cleric who became the ruler of Iran as Supreme Faqih, appointed new leaders and returned the country to Islamic law. Islamic centers were established, minority groups such as the Kurds and Azerbaijanis began uprisings all over the country, trying to gain autonomy, and, most shocking of all, fifty-two Americans in Iran were taken hostage.

And I, because my father was an Iranian, became the enemy at Odle Junior High in Bellevue, Washington. I remember several cocky twelve-year-old boys circling and teasing me one day in front of the girls' restroom. At first I thought it was a game but then realized that they really saw me as an adversary. Later a teacher stopped me in the hall to ask about my ethnicity. "I just heard you're Iranian," said Mr. Hiemdahl. "Is it really true?"

My younger brothers, still in elementary school, were cornered and harassed. Standing back to back, the two of them thwarted blows to the body but couldn't fend off biting, sarcastic comments. The experience jolted our self-esteem and the way we felt about our Middle Eastern heritage. One day, as I sat studying the kids in class, wondering about their backgrounds, I felt that nothing could be worse than being from Iran.

I remember my father and his Iranian friends huddled in front of the TV every night at the beginning of the revolution. The images frightened me—throngs of angry demonstrators in the tens of thousands, car bombs, machine guns, the burning of American flags, broken storefront windows, blindfolded American hostages. I couldn't identify with the fury in my father's country, a place I had lived for five years as a young child. For the first time, because of actions perpetrated five thousand miles away on another continent, shame and guilt joined the repertoire of my adolescent emotions. I recall thinking that as an Iranian, I was on the lowest rung of society. The only solace I found was comparing myself to a Russian girl in my class, thinking she was just as bad off as I was.

The Cold War and Communism, seen by Westerners as threats back then, have today been replaced by the threat of Muslim-backed terrorism and the supposed desire of these radical fundamentalists to conquer the West and bring it under the control of Islam.

> I couldn't identify with the fury in my father's country, a place I had lived for five years as a young child. For the first time, because of actions perpetrated five thousand miles away on another continent, shame and guilt joined the repertoire of my adolescent emotions.

My heart breaks to think of the millions of innocent Muslims battling the demons of prejudice and shame as I did as a young girl. Having traveled extensively as an adult and seen the injustices others have overcome, I no longer suffer from the same level of insecurity and self-loathing. Through the influence of incredible people as well as my faith in Christ, I've gained strength and confidence. When responding to circumstances like 9-11 and the war in Iraq, I keep in mind that there are two points of view to all such conflicts. And I try to understand both sides.

Muslims and Questions

Most Americans have become aware of the fact that Muslims are in our workplaces, our neighborhoods, and our communities. Perhaps you're wondering, like I have, how these Muslims are taking recent events involving Muslims on the national and world scene. You wonder if they share the beliefs of Muslims in the Middle East who say they are in a holy war to destroy Americans, "the infidels." You'd like to sit down with some Muslims here and find out just what they believe and how they feel about these anti-American attacks. But you don't want to communicate narrowmindedness or mistrust. You feel hesitant to go to a Muslim with your questions.

It's not easy deciphering the differing messages we have been given in this new war on terrorism that have so many references to Muslims and Arabs. The tide of unpopular opinion toward Muslims in America rose to new levels immediately after 9-11. I understand that most of the comments made initially were simply a reaction to the attacks. Since then, some leaders have apologized for their impulsive negative remarks about Muslims and their faith. I'm sure that most would now find more discerning ways to convey their concern about Muslim-backed terrorism in the West.

On many levels, Christian reaction to Muslim terrorism has been one of bitterness and resentment. Many Christians have uncritically, without doing any investigation or research, accepted as truth what they have read or heard about the beliefs and practices of Muslims. Reactions to attacks on American soil revealed deeply felt suspicions, sentiments never before articulated in public about the followers of Islam. Several Christian leaders described Islam as "evil" and "wicked." They claimed that Muslims want to control and, if need be, destroy our nation. Others said true Islam abhors violence. Perhaps you have heard similar remarks and are left wondering what to believe.

> Reactions to attacks on American soil revealed deeply felt suspicions, sentiments never before articulated in public about the followers of Islam.

A group of leading evangelical Christians, meeting in May 2003, condemned the derogatory statements about Islam made by several prominent religious leaders. Participants at the meeting said that scathing comments endanger the church's work in Islamic countries, strain interfaith dialogue, and feed the misguided belief that Christians are at war with Muslims. Hodan Hassan, a spokesperson for the Council of American-Islamic Relations, said, "We can understand theological differences, but what's important is that the dialogue is one of respect, not demonization."[1]

Who do we turn to for answers? Who are reliable sources of information about what seem to be Muslim agendas against the West? The media? Government leaders? Educators? Pastors?

Unfortunately, rather than digging for reliable answers to our questions about Muslims and Islam, it's simply easier to find answers on the evening news or on talk-radio programs. It's understandable to feel uncomfortable or timid about going to a Muslim directly to ask about the sensitive subject of Muslim anger toward the United States. We don't want to offend or pry. But our silence causes the chasm to widen. It divides us as neighbors and, ultimately, as a nation.

So often the human response to conflict is to focus on what separates people rather than looking at the things we share in common. How easy it is to judge others by their clothing, accent, skin coloring, or economic status. How easy it is to zoom in on the 20 percent of things we disagree with than on the 80 percent of things we agree on regarding the most fundamental issues in life. Christians living in the West may be surprised to learn that they have more in common with Muslims than they think.

The Door to Understanding

Most people know that myths are false ideas that are passed on as truths—by family, peers, and the media. Myths abound regarding Muslims and their Islamic faith. We too often naively accept as truth what is actually myth. Those who pass on such misinformation about Muslims may be sincere and believe that what they are saying is true. But the myths they pass on often produce fear, suspicion, and intolerance. Many of us accept these ideas without question and find ourselves driven farther from our Muslim neighbors. This is a concern for many Muslims living in the West who feel that they are not well represented and are often misjudged. They regret the fact that most Americans receive information about the Islamic faith and ideals through the narrow lens of biased media or religious institutions, not from practicing Muslims.

The Christian way to approach those of other faiths is in love (1 Cor. 13:13). Although I am the daughter of a Muslim father and a Catholic mother, it wasn't until I took some courses about Islam at the University of Washington and traveled to the Middle East that I began to address some of my own prejudices and began to look at Muslims with the eyes of love. Oftentimes I find that Western Christians are ignorant of the fact that Islam has many things in common with our Christian beliefs. Rather than pit our religious differences against one another, I have found it more beneficial to explore our commonalities as a springboard to the greater mysteries of the gospel.

In the following chapters, I will address some myths that are commonly held by Westerners. Perhaps you're wondering how pervasive these myths are. Am I making a mountain out of a molehill? Let me share a recent experience with you.

Melanie, a mother at my children's school, called me one afternoon. "Shirin, I just need to rant. I hope you don't mind."

"Sure," I replied. "Go ahead, fire." I was intrigued by the indignation in her tone.

As a volunteer curriculum coordinator, I was accustomed to having mothers call me from time to time with their questions and concerns regarding school curriculum. Melanie was upset about a history book that I had selected.

"Well, I just read the Muslim section in the kids' history book, and I can't believe what it says in there about Muslims being peace-loving people, believing in the same God we do, and that an angel came to Muhammad with a revelation from God. Everyone knows Muslims are not peace-loving people. Look what happened with 9-11. And they certainly don't believe in the same God we do. How can we let our kids read books like that in our Christian school?"

I quickly had questions of my own: How much did she really know about Islam? Would her tone have been different if she had known that my father is a Muslim? Was there anything in the reading that she could share with her children that would help them in understanding Muslims?

I took a deep breath and began to explain the merits of the history book, which simply portrays the Muslim faith the way that a Muslim would. Then I encouraged her to take the next step—to explain to her children how the Christian faith compares with the Muslim faith. I explained that the challenge would not be easy, because children can ask some tough questions about other religions. But I emphasized that we should not be giving our children a watered-down version of different religions and worldviews.

The Muslims living among us are grieved by the hate crimes that a small minority of Muslims half a world away perpetrate in the name of Islam. Muslims have come to this country with dreams for a better tomorrow. They believe in the promise of America. They love their children and desire to have peaceful, fruitful lives. And they are offended and hurt by the negative perceptions that so many Americans now have of their people.

Bernard Sabella, a Christian working among Palestinian refugees, reminds the church that all men are created in the image of God and that everyone, regardless of their background, is in the image of God, the Creator.

What Muslims and Christians Share in Common

As we teach our children about different faiths, such as Islam, I have found it helpful to first focus on the things we have in common. In the popular media, Muslims are often portrayed as militant religious fanatics. Most people are unaware that Muslims are actually as diverse in their beliefs as Christians are in theirs. Both Christendom and the Islamic world have believers who are polar opposites, those on the fundamental and conservative right and those on the liberal left.

Few Westerners know that Islam and Christianity agree on some major points of theology—a belief in prayer to God, spiritual disciplines such as fasting and giving to the poor, and a belief in personal holiness. Many Christians and Muslims condemn drunkenness, premarital sex, drug abuse, and abortion. As parents, for the benefit of our children, we can support one another on the PTA and in our communities. Together we can advocate that our adolescents dress modestly, treat adults respectfully, and avoid social situations which encourage promiscuity and delinquent behavior. Drawing on our similar spiritual beliefs, Christians and Muslims can forge friendships to make our communities safer and more honoring to God.

You may be asking, Where do I begin and how do I move toward Muslims in an educated, respectful manner? First, Westerners must have some knowledge of the practices of the Islamic faith in order to be more sensitive to the fact that Muslims are seeking God and have many of the same beliefs as Christians. In many respects, devout Christians may have more in common with devout Muslim colleagues and neighbors than they do with their secular, agnostic associates who support political agendas and lifestyles that are in opposition to biblical teachings. Following is a list of beliefs shared by Muslims and Christians.

- God is one, the creator of heaven and earth.

- God sent the Pentateuch, the Psalms, and the New Testament as his inspired Word.[2]

- All humans have sinned.

- Jesus was conceived by the Holy Spirit, without sin, in the womb of the Virgin Mary and lived a sinless life.

- Jesus is the Word of God.

- Jesus performed miracles, raised the dead, and healed the blind, the deaf, and the demon-possessed.

- Jesus will return again and will intercede for humans at the Last Judgment.

Beliefs That Are Different

We've noted that Christians and Muslims have some important things in common, but there's no hiding the fact that there are some profound areas of disagreement between us. Muslims have their own religious traditions and sacraments, which are different from Christian beliefs. Islam is founded on five pillars. Devout Muslims must make tremendous sacrifices to live out their faith based on the faith's five pillars. So Christians can admire their zeal to please God and be holy like him. Look with me briefly at what these five pillars are:

> Devout Muslims must make tremendous sacrifices to live out their faith based on the faith's five pillars. So Christians can admire their zeal to please God and be holy like him.

Pillar 1: Faith. Muslims believe that there is no God but Allah and that Muhammad is his prophet. According to Islam, Allah is the creator and therefore, by nature, all people are Muslims.

The Koran is God's message revealed through the angel Gabriel and given to Muhammad. The Bible is also considered a holy book. Adam, Noah, Abraham, Moses, and Jesus are all called prophets. Muhammad is said to be the last prophet, completing the message of the Old and New Testaments.

Pillar 2: Prayer. Muslims are instructed to pray five times a day. On Friday it is customary for followers to attend worship at a mosque, usually at noontime. Muslim law requires that worshipers, both young and old, men and women, whether in the Middle East or anywhere else in the world, answer the call to prayer and face their holy city of Mecca before sunrise, at noon, in the late afternoon, after sunset, and before bed.

Pillar 3: Fasting. Muslims fast from dawn to sunset each day for the entire month of Ramadan (the ninth lunar month) to commemorate Muhammad's receiving the Koran during Ramadan. Muslims refrain from drinking or eating during daylight hours. At sundown, families share a special meal together.

Pillar 4: Giving Alms. Muslims are taught to give alms for the poor each year. Islamic law states they must give anywhere from 2 to 10 percent of their income.

Pillar 5: Pilgrimage to Mecca. Allah decreed that Muslims are to travel to Mecca at least once in their lifetime, unless they are ill or very poor. The pilgrimage, called the *hajj,* is a time marked by special prayers and fellowship with other Muslims and guarantees believers their entrance to paradise. After the pilgrimage, a person receives the religious title of *hajji.*

Most important of the areas of disagreement are the issues related to the deity of Christ and his resurrection. Muslims believe that God is one, not a triune God as Christians believe, and that he is in many respects unknowable. Muslims do not easily understand the Trinity or the reason for the Cross, but many are open to discussing such points of theology. Much has been written about our differences. Many books treat this subject fairly and can help to equip you for a faith-based dialogue with Muslims. A few suggestions of books that can help you gain a better understanding of the Muslim faith are given below.

In the next chapter, we will look at the misconception that all Muslims are Arab. Learning how rich is the tapestry of Muslim ethnic groups around the world can help you to appreciate Muslims as individuals, each with their own history and culture, rather than lumping all Muslims together as one group.

QUESTIONS FOR REFLECTION AND DISCUSSION

1. What myths about Islam did you believe before reading this chapter?

2. Where can you find an English translation of the Koran and other literature that may help you inform yourself about Islam? Can you find it on the Internet? What might be some cautions to keep in mind when doing this research?

3. What are some ways your faith is apparent to Muslims with whom you may have contact?

4. How can you speak about your faith in Christ without offending a Muslim? Give some examples.

SUGGESTED READING

Accad, Foud Elias. *Building Bridges: Christianity and Islam*. Colorado Springs, Colo.: Navpress, 1997.

Adeney, Miriam. *Daughters of Islam*. Downers Grove, Ill.: InterVarsity Press, 2002.

Cragg, Kenneth. *The Call of the Minaret*. Nigeria: Day Star, 1985.

Marshall, Paul, Roberta Green, and Lela Gilbert. *Islam at the Crossroads: Understanding Its Beliefs, History, and Conflicts*. Grand Rapids: Baker, 2002.

Parshall, Phil. *Understanding Muslim Teachings and Traditions: A Guide for Christians*. Grand Rapids: Baker, 2002.

all Muslims
are Arab

When you're alone, you're
like a drop of water. But when
you're with your Muslim
friends, you're part of the sea,
one of many drops.

—ARAFEH, AN EGYPTIAN-
  PALESTINIAN, AT A MUSLIM
  GATHERING ON HER CAMPUS

A polished man in a charcoal-colored blazer and turtleneck sat beside me on a flight to Baltimore. He wore a Rolex watch and exuded the aroma of Calvin Klein cologne. He buckled his seat belt, pulled out his laptop, and responded to his emails. Once the plane took off, he shut his laptop, relaxed, and turned toward me in a friendly manner. We made small talk, inquiring about one another's travel plans and employment. He thought my name, Shirin, was unusual.

"Never heard it before," he said. "Does it mean anything?"

"Yes, my name is Iranian. It means 'sweet,' like candy, or the way you would describe something precious."

"Iranian, huh? Does that mean you speak Arabic?"

"No." I chuckled. "I speak Persian, the language spoken in my father's country, Iran. Arabic and Persian are very different languages, just as are English and German."

It's common for Westerners to lump together all people with a Middle Eastern background, assuming they are all Arabs and Muslims with a single language and culture. Yet the people of the Muslim world are as dissimilar as are the Portuguese, Dutch, and Romanians on the continent of Europe. In fact, the majority of Muslims live in Asia and Africa rather than in the Middle East. Currently in the United States, 42 percent of all Muslims are African-American, 24 percent are of South Asian origin, and 12 percent are of Arab descent.[1]

Islam expert Phil Parshall, in his book *Beyond the Mosque*, writes, "Diversity? Decidedly yes! This diversity at times leads to serious rifts in the unity of Islam. But cracks are not severances. The great rock of Islam remains cohesive. One can safely conclude that Islam is going to be around for a very long time."[2]

Some may have concluded that all Muslims are Arab after reading as a child fairy tales about sheiks, harems, and Aladdin's lamp or by watching Hollywood films like *Lawrence of Arabia*. We've all seen countless images on TV and in newspapers and magazines of Muslims with tan skin and dark eyes, men with beards and women in head scarves that reinforce this belief that all Muslims are Arabs. These images reflect some parts of Muslim life, but I want you to take a look at the whole picture with me.

From the drought-weary villages of Sudan in Africa to the cosmopolitan high-rises of Istanbul in Turkey to the rice fields of Western China, Muslims do not, in fact, share a common appearance or dialect or even the same religious beliefs. They reside in fifty countries worldwide, including the United States, and inhabit six different continents—a luxurious mix of nationalities, customs, and languages—all Muslim, each unique in their own way.

I am the daughter of an Irish-Catholic mother and an Iranian-Muslim father, which makes me a Muslim by birth. But I am a follower of Christ and attend a Protestant church. I'm nearly five feet, eleven inches tall and carry myself like an American. I dress like an American. But I have the slight bone structure and the exotic coloring of a Middle Eastern woman. Throughout my travels I've been mistaken as Greek, Italian, Turkish, and French. My family is Muslim, but we are not Arab.

The Arab World

Stretching more than four thousand miles across North Africa and the Middle East, from the Atlantic to the Indian oceans, is a conglomerate of nearly twenty independent nations, protectorates, sheikdoms, and other political units encompassed by a simple phrase—"the Arab World."[3] In simplest terms, Arabs are people who speak Arabic and originate from the Middle East or North Africa. The population of the Arab world is nearly three hundred million, of whom 92 percent are Muslim. Some Arabs are Christian. Others are Jewish.

The Arabic language is believed by Muslims to be the language of God. According to Islam, God chose Arabic to convey his message to the prophet Muhammad. Muslims consider the Arabic Koran to be the clearest and most reliable version because it is the language of God's revelation. All other versions are considered mere translations. Followers of Islam who live outside the Arab world are encouraged to learn to read and worship in Arabic.

Most Westerners believe that the majority of Muslims live in the Arab world. They are surprised to learn that in actuality, only 25 percent of the world's Muslims live in this area. Today more than 50 percent of Muslims live in Asia.[4] Central Asia, China, Bangladesh, Indonesia, and the Philippines are home to millions of Muslims. The largest concentration of Muslims in the world is in Indonesia, numbering 231 million.[5] Another 147 million Muslims live in Pakistan.[6]

And more Arab-speaking Christians, whose Palestinian-Christian ancestors helped to establish the New Testament church, live in America today than in Palestine.[7]

Islam in Asia and Europe

Sasha is from Central Asia. He has a square jaw and slanted eyes, the striking appearance of a modern-day Genghis Khan, the Mongol conqueror of the twelfth century. But Sasha, though he lives in the same area, speaks quietly and exudes all of the formality and politeness of a gentleman. He's a Muslim.

How did Muslims come to be in Central Asia? Arabs moved aggressively into these areas and brought about mass conversions to Islam by the fourteenth century. Commercial trading between China and Arab nations brought about the further spread of Islam to every province of that vast nation.

Today, many Chinese Muslims living in the West trace their ancestry to Arabs, Persians, or the Turks. I learned this while on holiday in Turkey when I showed some Tatar Muslims (Tatar Muslims live in Central Asia, near Mongolia) a photograph of a Chinese-American friend back home. Suddenly one of the young Tatars pulled the picture up to his face and pointed to the eyes of my friend, showing me that their eyes were the same.

Six republics of the former Soviet Union—Azerbaijan, Kazakhstan, Kyrgyzstan, Tajikistan, Turkmenistan, and Uzbekistan—are Muslim countries. Albania, Kosovo, and Slovenia are also home to followers of Islam. Immigrating to the West from these lands are blonde and blue-eyed Muslims, dark-haired oriental-looking Muslims, and a combination of both.

> Muslims bear no one look, identifying feature, or manner of attire. Muslims are rich and poor, educated and illiterate, bigoted and open-minded, deeply spiritual and secular, just as are the people of any other major religion.

Muslims bear no one look, identifying feature, or manner of attire. Muslims are rich and poor, educated and illiterate, bigoted and open-minded, deeply spiritual and secular, just as are the people of any other major religion.

Increasingly, Muslims who live in the West are the children of immigrant parents or grandparents. Often these first- and second-generation children feel estranged from Islam. They are the university students and young professionals among us who are alienated from their religion but still feel a bond to their heritage.

Bicultural Children Seek Identity

"We're schizophrenics," said Yasmin, who was born and raised in France, and who is the oldest of six children whose parents are Muslims. "At home we learn about Islam. At school we learn about the world. We don't have cultural codes as do other Muslims who live in Muslim countries."

As the daughter of bicultural parents, I identify with Yasmin. We look foreign, but inside we think and feel like other Westerners. The life of children growing up with Muslim parents in the West is perplexing. All we want is to fit in with both of our worlds. Sadly, as bicultural people, we're not entirely accepted in either culture, and we bump along through life, trying to figure out what's right and wrong and to avoid earning our parents' scorn.

Yasmin's reflections remind me of the many misunderstandings I've encountered as the daughter of an Iranian father and an American mother. Like most children with parents from two different countries, my identity seems to shift, depending on the circumstances. At times it can feel like I have a split personality. Depending on the situation, I may need to act more Middle Eastern—to be submissive, to placate, bargain, or otherwise manipulate circumstances in my favor. At other times I am more like many Americans—gregarious, aggressive, and unabashedly self-confident. It's a convoluted and at times thrilling experience to navigate life in such a manner, kind of like driving two remote-control race cars at the same time. And, to be honest, I'd have it no other way.

Visiting My Muslim Father's Homeland

Muslim children in the United States often find travel to the country of origin of their Muslim parents difficult. Naively, I had promised my father that I would visit Iran with my husband and two small children. What I learned was that the Revolution of 1979 in Iran had made it impossible for me to enter Iran with my American passport.

I was living in France at the time because of a work assignment. I remember standing in line at the Iranian consulate in Paris behind a petite woman who was wearing a black head scarf and dark, long raincoat. She looked uncomfortably warm, constantly securing her scarf on her head, as we both nervously waited to speak to the stern man behind the bulletproof window.

I was tense, wondering how many more trips I would have to make to the consulate before I would be permitted to travel to Tehran, in Iran. I had lived in Iran for five years as a child but had not been back in twenty-three years. Little did I know how my sense of identity would be tested.

Large portraits of religious leaders, including Muhammad and the Ayatollah Khomeini, hung on the walls. The lobby floor was marble and granite. At five different counters, men and women politely, in hushed tones, pleaded their cases with Iranian government officials.

That afternoon, I learned that to fly to Iran I would need an Iranian passport. I also learned that my husband could not travel with me because we were not considered legally married under Islamic law. *Great, now I'm an adulterer and have illegitimate children*, I thought to myself. My Christian wedding ten years earlier in Seattle, Washington, was not recognized because I was the daughter of an Iranian-Muslim man. "Certainly there's some misunderstanding," I pleaded. "I was born in the U.S., my mother was American, and I was raised Christian."

> My Christian wedding ten years earlier in Seattle, Washington, was not recognized because I was the daughter of an Iranian-Muslim man.

"No," said the man with dark razor stubble and a white collarless shirt. He frowned. "If you travel to Iran, you must travel as an Iranian. You don't have the rights of a Christian unless you go to Iran and register yourself as a Christian. Your marriage in the U.S. is invalid. Therefore it's against the law for you to travel with a man inside Iran."

Anger enveloped me. *I already am a Christian*, I thought. "Converting to Christianity," as they called it, could land in me in jail—or worse—in an Islamic country. What century did we live in? How could the official say such things in Paris, one of the most secular and democratic cities in the world? Couldn't they see that I was different, not completely like them? I left the consulate stunned, my resolve to travel to Iran as dampened as the drizzly Parisian weather.

Several months later, my father, while visiting France, escorted me to the consulate to plead my case again. Maybe things would turn out differently this time, I told myself. "I would like my son-in-law and grandchildren to visit me in Iran," my father said to the government worker. "Surely you can appreciate our wishes. Could you grant them some kind of an exception? My daughter is thirty-three years old and has been married for ten years. Her mother baptized her Catholic. Her situation is unique."

The official shook his head. "You're Iranian. You're Muslim. There-fore your daughter is Muslim. She cannot travel to Iran with her hus-band unless they perform a Muslim wedding here at the consulate. There are no exceptions."

"Please try to understand," my father said, trying again. "You can't apply the same rules to her as you would to someone living inside Iran."

"No! I can't help you. The rules must be followed."

"Well, how will she ever become a Muslim if we treat her like this?" my father shot back, losing all patience. "You really need to be thinking about the younger generation and how all of this affects them."

We left the embassy, heartbroken. In the following months, I per-sisted in my efforts to secure an Iranian passport and eventually resigned to traveling to Iran alone. The risks were simply too high for my husband and children. In April, eleven months after I first began applying for Iranian travel documents, I nervously boarded the plane that would take me from London to Tehran. I had my new Iranian passport in hand. I knew it was risky. Some American friends tried to discourage me from going. "What if you can't get out?" they asked. "The rules in that coun-try are different for women."

Prior to my departure, my husband had called the American embassy and discovered I would be forfeiting my American rights while visiting Iran without my American passport. In Iran I would be consid-ered a single woman in need of my father's protection and consent to enter and leave the country. If anything were to happen to my father while I was in Iran, I would have no one to turn to, no way to quickly exit the country.

I wondered if I was gambling too much by traveling to Iran alone. I remembered the difficul-ties experienced by Betty Mah-moody, who was married to an Iranian and tried to leave Iran with her daughter. She wrote about her experiences in her book *Not without My Daughter*. Once again I felt confused about my identity. Was my strong Middle Eastern sense

> Once again I felt confused about my identity. Was my strong Middle Eastern sense of family loyalty going to cost me more than I was willing to pay?

of family loyalty going to cost me more than I was willing to pay? I pushed the fears back and prayed for courage, trusting God for my choices and safety. I have never felt more terrified in my life.

All fears were put to rest when I arrived in Iran and my relatives celebrated my homecoming as if I were a young bride. Each night elegant dinner parties were held in my honor. I was showered with gifts. My father enjoyed having me all to himself. I left the country a week later unscathed except for a touch of food poisoning, nothing more.

Using my hidden American passport, I flew back to Charles De Gaulle Airport in Paris and, with new eyes, was reunited with my blue-eyed, fair-colored children and husband. The land of my father seemed light-years and worlds apart from my life in Paris. I marveled at my complex identity and how little my children would ever comprehend the hurdles I have had to overcome in being a bicultural person. With an American father and American passports, they will never see the world through two different sets of lenses, as I do. Nor will they know the heartache of feeling strangely set apart, not fully a citizen of either culture.

Understanding Disconnected Muslims

How do Muslims view their lives in the West? How do they see themselves? According to a 1999 *Current Psychology* report, which examined societal influences on gender identity, Arab-American girls feel greater ties to their Muslim heritage than do boys.[8] Three-fourths of the girls, ranging in age from thirteen to eighteen, characterized themselves as Middle Eastern. Fewer boys did. Another study, completed in 1996, examined the factors which contribute to the identity of Muslim girls born to immigrant parents and raised in the United States.[9] Analysis of the data suggests that the girls lived very different lives at home and at school and often felt as if they were viewing life from the sidelines, not fully accepted at school or at home. Neither educators nor parents seemed fully equipped to help bicultural children embrace with confidence their multifaceted identities.

Zadie Smith's novel *White Teeth* beautifully illustrates the dysfunction and undeniable love between two Muslim parents living with their sons in London. The two brothers of Indian descent choose very different paths for their lives. One prefers the Muslim gangs of London and a series of loveless relationships with adolescent girls who find his dark looks breathtaking. The other chooses a safe scholarly life. The sons bring their parents both delight and heartache. The parents miss India but prefer their life in the West, even though at times it seems joyless, to the war, famine, and disease back home. Reading Smith's work, one can empathize with the complexity of growing up in a culture that is not your parents' and the pain of raising children who may never embrace your deeply rooted values and religion.

Growing up in Bellevue, Washington, so close to Boeing and Microsoft, I felt that my world was very different from that of my American peers. I grew up hearing and speaking both English and Persian. I entertained my friends in a living room filled with Persian carpets, samovars, hand-painted vases, and ancient water pipes. We ate Campbell's soup chicken casserole one night, lamb kabobs on the grill the next, and fish on Fridays during Lent. We attended Catholic religious education classes on Wednesday afternoons. On Sunday mornings we went to Mass with our mother. My Muslim father was gone much of the time. When he was home, I saw him pray, but he did not attend a mosque. In raising his children, he did not speak of religious teachings. But I know now that as he supervised my appearance and my behavior, frowning on my makeup and phone calls from boys at school, he was expressing his Muslim orientation and was trying to be a good Muslim. I did my best to keep everyone happy.

Images of my childhood would remind most Westerners of the hit comedy My Big Fat Greek Wedding. Amusing as they may appear at first, the lives of bicultural children are complicated, leaving many feeling awkward about their ethnicity and unsure of their place in society. Many feel tugged at and pulled in different directions linguistically, religiously, intellectually, or socially by parents and by their Western culture.

Some grow up in a state of cultural confusion, never really understanding why they have such peculiar parents and wishing they had been raised in a "normal" American family instead. They ask themselves, "Why don't my parents understand me? Why can't they help me more with my homework? Why aren't they as enthusiastic about my basketball games as are American parents? Why can't we have a Christmas tree or Easter eggs? Why is my dad so strict about dating?" As a young person, it can be painful to feel left out when you don't have the same privileges as your peers because your parents value other things instead. Many never learn their parents' language or their parents' worldview. For most, it may require a trip to their parents' country of origin or several college-level international-studies courses to be able to understand the complexity of their own backgrounds.

Many bicultural Muslim youth feel a spiritual chasm in their lives. With no formal religious education, they are open to friendships with Christians who can help answer life's questions and introduce them to a community which oftentimes feels like an extended family.

> Many bicultural Muslim youth feel a spiritual chasm in their lives. With no formal religious education, they are open to friendships with Christians who can help answer life's questions and introduce them to a community which oftentimes feels like an extended family.

Most bicultural people eventually learn to manage life gracefully and many even learn to thrive, developing a skill set perfect for a global economy. "I consider myself lucky to have been exposed to both cultures," says Necva Ozgur, a Turkish woman and school principal in Pasadena, California. "My children have close ties to their relatives in Istanbul. In the U.S., individuality is respected. I enjoy my privacy and solitude, the freedom of the press and political expression."

Muslims born in the West tend to feel little connection with their religion and are hurt when they are lumped together with Muslim fundamentalist and radical groups abroad. Most appreciate it when you take the time to inquire about their ethnicity rather than assuming they belong to a specific group of Muslims. They are proud of their heritage and desire to pass on noteworthy traditions and beliefs to the next generation.

In the next chapter we'll examine the sensitive issue of Muslim hatred toward the West.

QUESTIONS FOR REFLECTION AND DISCUSSION

1. Can you think of any false stereotypes you have seen about Muslims in the popular media? Give some examples.

2. Do you have any bicultural friends or acquaintances? If so, what are some observations you have made about them?

3. How are they like you? How are they different? What are some of their struggles? What are some of their strengths?

4. What are some ways that you can show an interest in Muslims in your area?

all Muslims
hate the West

All cultures are liable to a healthy
jealousy for their own identity with a
lively suspicion of an alien intrusion
into their own proper responsibility.

—KENNETH CRAGG, *THE CALL OF THE MINARET*

I often watch the evening news with a familiar sense of horror. The images are all too brutal. A scarved woman beats her chest, mourning over the dead body of her teenage son. A middle-aged man wipes blood off his forehead after receiving a blow to the temple by rock-throwing adolescents. A maimed girl is briskly carried away on a stretcher after a bombing in a wedding salon. A gathering of unshaven males viciously burns an American flag while cursing the "Great Satan."

Familiar? Must be the Middle East, right? Media reporting from that part of the world shows a turbulent, war-infested Third World catastrophe, and Muslims as angry vigilantes, deploring anything remotely related to modern Western civilization. But what is captured with a camera rarely tells the whole story. Though conflict is a reality for many living in the Middle East, I challenge you to consider an insider's point of view that reveals details of what led to the myth that all Muslims hate the West.

Whether traveling in Cyprus, Iran, Jordan, or Uzbekistan, I've discovered that Muslims are friendly to and curious about Westerners, even to the point of infatuation. Even today, the "man on the street" is friendly to friendly Americans. During my travels as a student, and later in my work as a university chaplain among international students, I've met hundreds of Muslims and never been treated unjustly or with hostility. If anything, as an American I've been shown the highest of respect.

When I was in Dushanbe, the capital of Tajikistan, a dozen young girls with long braids and colorful oriental clothing giddily circled me one summer afternoon. They were delighted to meet an American and hear me speak Persian, like they do. They begged my American travel companions and me to join them at a tea house, so we spent the afternoon sitting on Persian carpets, sipping tea. The girls had so many questions: What is life like back in the United States? What did we do for fun? Would we please come back and visit again? We ended our time with warm embraces, exchanging addresses and the hope that our paths would one day cross again.

In Istanbul, Turkey, two years later, after an American-Turkish exchange outing, a number of students pushed their phone numbers into the palm of my hand, begging me to call them. "I'd like you to come to my house for dinner," Hulya pleaded. "I want my parents to meet you. I'd like to take you to the Grand Bazaar sometime." As an American exchange student, I found it difficult to manage my busy social calendar while living among Muslims. My year abroad turned into an endless cycle of dinner invitations, sightseeing excursions, and tutoring sessions with students eager to perfect their English skills. I also attended a small church with Turkish Christians.

I adore the look of Muslims' eyes lighting up when Westerners show a genuine interest in them. With childlike fascination, they are curious about Americans, Canadians, and the British. It is considered an honor to invite a Westerner into their home. Whether rich or poor, given the chance, the majority of Muslims would gladly lavish a guest from the West with hospitality and would be delighted to number him or her among their friends. Many, in fact, would jump at the opportunity to visit or live in any of our open and prosperous nations.

A Muslim's interest in all things "American," however, is distinctly separate from his political views and his religious identity. According to

Kenneth Cragg, author of *The Call of the Minaret,* Christians, in particular, must be careful to not offend Muslims concerning their place in
the world: "Christians must bring a wide and warm understanding. Not
deploring that their task is difficult, they must undertake cheerfully the
burden of being on many counts suspect. Is it to be wondered at if a
Christian of British or U.S. origin encounters obstacles in ministry
among [Muslims]? Would it not be surprising were it otherwise, given
the legacies of a century?"[1]

Historical Basis of Conflict

Conflict between Muslim and Christian powers dates back to the Middle Ages. Within a century of Muhammad's death, Islam had conquered
most of the Christian lands in the Near East and the better part of North
Africa, Spain, and parts of France.[2] During this Golden Age of Islam,
people from a plethora of races and creeds were converted to Islam.

But the advancement of Islam did not go unchecked. In 800 A.D.
"Charlemagne advanced into Spain marking the limit of expansion of
Islam into Western Europe. Thereafter, the pattern was one of retreat in
the west, but improved advance in the east," writes Edward Mortimer,
an Islamic specialist, in his book *Faith and Power: The Politics of Islam.*[3]
The greatest blow to Muslim expansion came in the thirteenth century
when many Muslim strongholds fell to Mongol invaders. Some historians argue that Muslims never fully recovered and have experienced a
decline in their civilization ever since.

In more recent times, Muslims have a long history of feeling
encroached upon by Western powers. Mortimer writes:

> During the nineteenth century, the British completed the con-
> quest of India, Burma, and Malaysia, the Dutch of Indonesia, the Rus-
> sians of the Caucasus and Turkistan. British power, expanding from
> India, established itself at Aden [in what is now Yemen] and in the
> Persian Gulf. Three times British troops invaded Afghanistan, while
> Russian troops on several occasions occupied parts of northern Iran.
> In Africa, France seized Algeria in 1830. Expanding from there and
> from the former slave-trading settlements dotted along the Atlantic
> coast, she proceeded to subdue all the central Sahara and most of

Muslim-populated territory in West and Equatorial Africa. France occupied Tunisia in 1881. Britain occupied Egypt in 1882 and in 1890 moved up the Nile into Sudan. Spain expanded footholds in Morocco and Western Sahara, but the main part of Morocco came under French influence in 1912.[4]

Europeans continued to control the region. In 1916 a secret pact was signed dividing the territory of the former Ottoman Empire, which was supporting Germany in World War I, among Britain, France, and Russia. After the war, instead of granting independence to the Arab provinces as Britain had promised, Britain and France set up protectorates and mandates. Palestine came under the jurisdiction of the British. France took over what is now Syria and Lebanon. The new Soviet Union took over Muslim lands in Central Asia, the Balkans, and Russia. Only Turkey was able to establish itself as an independent state.

After World War II, with the approval of the United Nations, land was taken from Palestinians to establish a homeland for the Jews. At the time, Jews owned 6 percent of the land but were given 53.5 percent of Palestine in the partition plan.[5] The Zionist movement had spawned the belief that the creation of the physical state of Israel in Palestine was the fulfillment of biblical prophesies. Immigration by Jews to the Holy Land had started in the early part of the twentieth century. But after the partition of Palestine and Israel's declaration of independence, neighboring Arab countries and Arab Palestinians tried to take back the land and reclaim all of Palestine. The war lasted almost twenty months. During that time, hundreds of thousands of Palestinians became refugees, losing their land and their homes.

The Roots of Terrorism

The style of terrorist attack that has become so persistent in today's world had its roots in the 1940s, when the land was taken from Palestinians to establish a homeland for the Jews. Louis Hamada, in his book *Understanding the Arab World*, writes:

When British rule was coming to an end in Palestine, both the Arabs and the Jews practiced terrorism against one another, and against the British. Jewish terrorists killed 338 British citizens in Palestine during the 1940s. They blew up King David Hotel, the British headquarters in Jerusalem, in 1946, killing ninety-one persons, and perfected the lethal letter bomb.... The important point here, I think, is that Arabs don't have a patent on terrorism.... When the U.S. shells Muslim villages near Beirut or bombs Libyan terrorist targets, killing civilians in the process, Washington may view the act as one of retribution, but those on the receiving end surely consider it terrorism.[6]

Hamada says the Palestinians are still fighting the "illegal seizure and occupation of Palestine by the European Jews." He says their anger has been fueled by Israel's "mounting treacherous treatment of Palestinians."[7]

While living abroad for several years, I became accustomed to living with terrorism. I commonly saw armed patrols and bomb-sniffing dogs at European airports and train stations. I thought nothing of being frisked by officials while traveling into countries like Cyprus or Iran. I remember avoiding the Metro in Paris in the mid-1990s because of a series of bombings on the train lines. One Friday several American students we had been hosting in Paris for an exchange program left a train just minutes before a bomb went off. That same week another bomb killed seven Parisians and injured dozens. Algerian terrorists, angry about France's occupation in their country, took credit for the bombings. That summer changed the lives of these American students as they learned to live with terrorism just as many others, throughout the world, had already done.

The events of September 11 ushered all Americans into a new era—terrorism in our homeland. We had finally caught up with the rest of the world. I remember seeing images of the Twin Towers engulfed in flames and thinking, *Now it's our turn*.

Unfortunately many Western Christians are unfamiliar with the fact that today's Muslim-backed terrorism is in many respects related to the anger and injustice felt by Muslims toward the nation of Israel and our government's support of Israel.

Hamada writes, "Christians have been conditioned by Western political theology to support Israel's exclusive claim to the land of Palestine, and countless pulpits are being used as launch pads to promote the financial and political support of Israel."[8]

Before 9-11, terrorism on U.S. soil seemed incomprehensible even though people in Europe, North Africa, and the Middle East were living with such tensions every day.

Before 9-11, terrorism on U.S. soil seemed incomprehensible even though people in Europe, North Africa, and the Middle East were living with such tensions every day.

The Discovery of Oil and Western Decadence

Perhaps nothing has changed the course of the Muslim world's relationship with the West more than the discovery of oil. After World War II, the desert lands of the Middle East suddenly became a booming channel for petroleum wealth and the beginning of modern civilization. This in turn thrust open the doors to the West, bringing about dramatic changes. Westerners were needed to provide the leadership and capability to run the oil industry. With the Westerners came the introduction of Western goods and pleasures. Harry St. John Bridger Philby describes many of the changes in 1955:

> The once forbidden charms of music were openly paraded on the palace square, or blared in the face of the monarch, who sickened at the sound. The forbidden cinema reared its ogling screen in the scores in princely palaces and wealthy mansions to flaunt the less respectable products of Hollywood before audiences which would have blushed or shuddered at the sights but ten or fifteen years ago. Liquor and drugs have penetrated, more or less discretely, into quarters where, in the old days, people had been slain on sight for the crime of smoking tobacco, which has now become a substantial source of State revenue. Even seclusion of women has been tempered to the prevailing breeze of modernism.[9]

Many Muslims began to question such changes. What role would Islam play during times of rapid modernization? How could the Muslim world so easily forsake its past and embrace modern civilization? What would be the cost to their national and religious identity? Foreigners and their goods were flooding their countries, profoundly disturbing the balance of the Islamic world.

Taking Back Ground

The tide began to turn when local men in the oil-rich Middle East were employed and learned highly skilled jobs in the petroleum industry. With this knowledge came the power to change the division of profits between the Western oil companies and their host countries, securing 50 percent of the profits for the nationals. In 1960, when the oil preserves of the Middle East were estimated at 60 percent of the world's reserves, the main producing countries came together and formed the Organization of Petroleum Exporting Countries (OPEC).[10] This alliance enabled the oil-producing countries to form a common front in negotiations with Western oil companies. Eventually the countries took over the entire production side of the operation.

In time, along with the production of oil, some positive changes and amenities were introduced by Westerners living and working in the Middle East. They wanted better schools for their children and better hospitals. Farms, banks, highways, hotels, factories, and parks also were added during this period. Landowners were able to take a larger part of the oil profits and improved the Middle Eastern way of life. Merchants were able to purchase imports to expand the country's economic growth. Collaboration between Eastern and Western capitalists grew to a new level. For the first time public utilities—banks, railways, telephones, water, gas, and electricity—were taken into public ownership.[11]

With empowerment came a movement of nationalization, and the momentum sparked the desire to remove foreigners so that full control could go to the oil producers. Western foreigners began to leave, and the ruling class had new problems on their hands. A great disparity grew between rich and poor. Those who dominated the oil industry dominated the wealth structure. Like spoiled children in a candy store, they spent their wealth on their own pleasures rather than caring for the poor, the orphaned, the illiterate, the sick, and the religiously starved. They claimed they wanted the best for their people: peace, order, economic freedom, and a regime that would benefit all classes, but they never took serious measures to make a difference. By the mid-1980s, the leaders in these oil-rich countries were out of touch with their people. They also had failed to adopt good business practices for the production of the oil and its sale in a global economy. The united front of OPEC was crumbling.

As Islamic unity deteriorated, these divisions produced the breeding ground for fundamentalist groups that promised justice to the weary.

America's Role

But where did the animosity against Americans originate?

It's helpful to know that for the better part of our history, North America and the Middle East have been on friendly terms. But the relationship shifted after World War II. Many Muslims believe that America abandoned the relationship when the United States supported Israel's political aspirations and disregarded the many losses suffered by the Palestinians.

Louis Bahajat Hamada, author of *Understanding the Arab World*, says that America has provoked Muslims to wrath by taking sides with Israel while turning a deaf ear to the Arabs.

I don't share all of the views of my Muslim friends, but it helps to understand their side of the story.

The American Pro-Israel Stance

Why can't we see both sides?

Because the United States blindly supports Israel against the Palestinians, says Arab-world expert Hamada. America's pro-Israel stance is rooted in a Zionist movement dating back to World War II that succeeded in carving out a homeland for the Jews on Palestinian land. Muslim Arabs will never support this transfer of land to Israel because they believe millions of innocent Palestinians were displaced from their homes, from land which their ancestors had occupied for centuries. Christian Arabs living in the region also disagree with what was done. They witness the plight of their Palestinian neighbors, both Muslim and Christian, and have drawn their own conclusions about the Israeli-Palestinian conflict, conclusions that are quite different from the view of Christians in the West.

Jason, an American missionary who works among the Palestinians, fears that the fighting and suffering will not cease until the United States examines its one-sided support of Israel in the conflict. Jason and his family have sacrificed the comfort and safety of life in the United States to minister among Arab youth. He wants to make a difference among the emerging generation of Palestinians. But when he returns to Los Angeles on furlough, he often is saddened by the ignorance of many of his American friends regarding the Israeli-Palestinian conflict. "They simply can't identify with the Arab point of view, why the occupation of Israel in their homeland bothers the Palestinians so much. We see images of angry Arabs on TV, but we can't empathize with how they feel, intruded upon by Israel, and the deep bitterness that produces in the souls of their people."

It's not difficult to see how Muslims can look back on the last two hundred years of their history, especially the years since the end of World War II, and feel injured by such catastrophes to their religion and territory. It should come as no surprise that Muslims have mixed feelings about their relationship with countries like Great Britain and the United States.

Muslims respect many of the ideals and advances of modern Western civilization: freedom of speech, freedom of worship, human rights, entrepreneurialism, socialized medicine, and democracy. Given the opportunity, most desire to tap into the sources of Western ingenuity to strengthen their own societies.

But there remain some elements of Western values and ideals that keep them at arm's length and, at times, provoke them to anger. As author and journalist Philip Yancey says, "We think of ourselves as generous, compassionate, good-natured, slow to anger and committed to justice. Some overseas see us as arrogant, selfish, decadent and uncaring."[12] Accordingly, Muslims often have disdain for Western forms of entertainment, our sometimes brutish military might, and some of our choices for contributions in foreign aid.

Islam's Place in the World

Yet through all of the takeover by others, Muslims have continued to remain faithful to their religion. Where does this Muslim pride originate? Why do they feel so passionate about their role in the world? Ask any Muslim on the street, whether nominal or devout in matters of religion, and you'll find a Muslim who believes that Islam is the highest and final religion. A Muslim believes Islam regulates civilization and provides an ideal social system for the community of believers. Muslims see the role of their faith as the "the House of Islam"—a mighty fortress which surrounds all domains of life. From the seventh through the twelfth centuries, Islam supported many great advances in astronomy and architecture, in medicine and literature, art and philosophy.

But Islam also has a history of war and aggression, of which many Muslims in the West, particularly those born in our country, know little about. According to Dave Phillips, a campus minister to international students, Muslim parents tend to pass down the good and bypass the darker stories of the past. "They never mention the Christian youths persecuted by Muslims and forced to convert and become the Janissaries during the Ottoman Empire," Phillips says. "They never mention the hundreds of thousands of Armenians killed in Turkey in 1915. Even today they ignore the Khartoum government [in the Sudan, in Africa] which imposes the Shari'a law on Christian black tribes in the south through starvation and military attacks."

Because Muslims see history differently than we do, they have drawn some different conclusions. Phillips says Muslims believe their religion is peace-loving because they do not know about the atrocities of the past. They pride themselves that Islam historically has shown great tolerance and compassion toward Jews and Christians. They believe that there has never been anything like an Islamic inquisition or holocaust. Throughout the centuries, they say, Islamic countries welcomed Jews who fled the persecution of Christendom. But in the aftermath of 9-11, Phillips says, not enough Muslim leaders clearly condemned the attacks on American soil.[13]

With remarkable determination, average Muslims, even under the disgrace of 9-11, stand by their faith. They believe the war on the West was perpetrated by a minority of radical fundamentalists and that the majority of Muslims want to live in peace, following Muslim ideals. They prefer to believe that the true ideals of Islam—world peace, tolerance, unity, and love toward all mankind—have not yet been carried out. They cling to the hope that one day Islam will triumph over all other systems of belief as a global theocracy.

Western-Style Democracy Rejected

This means that some Muslims reject democracy and follow instead their religious leaders. Most Westerners would be dumbfounded to know that countries like Egypt, Jordan, Pakistan, and even Turkey, if given the opportunity to have free, democratic elections, would vote for religious extremists. Muslims worry that in countries like Iraq and Afghanistan, the United States won't allow the people to pick their own leaders. They do not want the United States to dictate the leaders they should have. They want to govern themselves.

Mahmood, who is from Iran but lives in the United States, was watching the evening news with his neighbor after the major combat of the war in Iraq had ended in 2003. The report turned to America's difficulty in promoting the ideals of democracy in the Arab country. The neighbor shook his head in disbelief and sighed. "Jeez, why can't they just get their act together?"

Mahmood was angered by the remark but waited to vent until after his neighbor had left. "He doesn't get it," he told his daughter. "Americans just don't get it, do they? The rebuilding of Iraq is not going to be some easy democratic process. So much work must be done first. Iraqis must learn about personal freedom and responsibility first. They'd turn to a religious government like Iran's before they'd become democratic like the U.S."

According to Milton Viorst, author of *In the Shadow of the Prophet: The Struggle for the Soul of Islam*, Muslims not only reject our occupation of Islamic nations such as Iraq and Afghanistan but also dismiss our Western-style democracy.

That dismissal of democracy goes back to the thirteenth century, when Muslims were enjoying their Golden Age. They had access to the writings of the ancient Greek philosophers—Socrates, Aristotle—who spawned the ideals of democracy.

Viorst writes, "Under the influence of the texts from ancient Greece, Muslims in their Golden Age considered and rejected these ideas [of democracy] before passing the texts on to Europe. After triggering the

Renaissance, the ideas led, over quarrelsome centuries, to the Reformation, the Enlightenment, and the Scientific Revolution. While Islam remained devoted to desert traditions, Europe created civilizations imbued with a sense of individual identity. These ideals, for better or worse, became the foundation of secular culture that characterizes Western civilization. This process has largely bypassed Islamic society."[14]

Muslims continue to have an entirely different worldview than Westerners. Whether we realize it or not, our values and outlook on life have largely been determined by a thousand years of teaching and indoctrination that led to our modern democracy. As a result, we're comfortable with our individuality, our separation of church and state, and the notion of a personal relationship with God. Muslims, on the other hand, are known for saying, "Islam isn't just a religion; it's a way of life." For them, there is no barrier between everyday life and faith. Religion impacts all levels of life. In Islam, every domain, whether religious or social, is under the watchful eye of God and his clergy.

Some Muslims now worry that since 9-11, Westerners perceive them differently than in the past. Muslim youth living in the United States, especially, are affected by this concern. An Arab mother, in an article in the *Los Angeles Times* in May 2003, recounts the fears her children have of arbitrary arrest.

"Can they send you to another place and have you tortured?" the young boy asked his mother.

"Absolutely not!" the mother assured him.

"Well, what if they make a mistake and you get taken to jail even though you didn't do anything wrong? I mean what if they sent you to jail just because of being Muslim? Everyone thinks Muslims are terrorists and bad people."

The boy's fears disturbed the mother. She knows it's now a reality for Muslims living in the United States to be taken into custody and held indefinitely in the war on terrorism. Though her children are proud of their Palestinian heritage, they see themselves primarily as Americans. The mother didn't have the heart to tell her sons that one day their security as Muslims living in the United States, even as citizens by birth, may be at risk.

At present, Muslims are threatened by the prejudice toward Muslims and Arabs that is festering in the hearts of many Americans. A Christian Zionist, according to Hamada, is a person who is more interested in helping God fulfill his prophetic plan through the physical and political Israel than in helping to give a person a chance to know the saving grace of Jesus Christ.

I've come to realize that ordinary Muslims don't hate Americans any more than ordinary Russians hated Americans during the Cold War. Having traveled among both peoples during times of political strain between the United States and their respective countries, I've found that the average man on the street is still

> A Christian Zionist, according to Hamada, is a person who is more interested in helping God fulfill his prophetic plan through the physical and political Israel than in helping to give a person a chance to know the saving grace of Jesus Christ.

very much infatuated with America. The images we see in the press of crowds of Muslims spewing hate for Americans are often a setup. While traveling in Iran, I learned that it's regular practice for propaganda buses, arranged for by the hard-liner Muslim press, to roll into small villages and round up the unemployed and pay them a day's wages to whip themselves up into an anti-American demonstration—beating their chests, waving their fists, and burning flags. The images are familiar and in many cases have been choreographed to fan the flames of Muslim militancy against the West.

Most Muslims I know in the United States and in the Middle East simply shake their heads in tired disgust, wishing we could all get on with our lives more peacefully. They're tired of the tensions between the West and the East. Yes, they have qualms about issues related to the Israeli-Palestinian conflict, as well as Western morality reflected in media and materialism. They at times are suspicious of the West's apparent desire to dominate the world's oil industry. But they would no sooner give up their Western citizenship than they would give up their Muslim faith.

Fortunately, now at the beginning of the twenty-first century, many Christians are traveling more and becoming more sensitive to other cultures. They want to understand other worldviews and what fuels the conflicts in difficult areas of the world. As a result, a number of Western Christians are now learning to love Palestinians and to empathize with their sense of injustice. Today, as Christians, we can see Palestinian Muslims not as enemies of Israel but rather as angry, displaced people whose homeland has been taken from them.

Let us grab this unique opportunity to befriend one another and pray for healing and the love of Christ to strengthen our nation. Remember the words of the apostle Paul, "If it is possible, as far as it depends on you, live at peace with everyone" (Rom. 12:18).

Living at peace doesn't mean we water down our beliefs and spiritual convictions. It does mean that we avoid words and actions that offend and end the relationship.

In the next chapter, we'll explore the myth that Muslim women are oppressed by Islam. This issue has awakened the interest and concern of many groups toward the plight of the poor and abused in the Muslim world. What you'll learn is that there is much diversity among Muslim women.

QUESTIONS FOR REFLECTION AND DISCUSSION

1. What kinds of images have you seen in the media that cause you to feel that Muslims hate Westerners?

2. What elements of Western life may be offensive to Muslims in your town?

3. Have you been influenced by the Christian Zionist movement? If so, how?

4. What aspects of the Muslims' relationship and history with the West discussed in this chapter were new to you? Did anything surprise you or make you angry?

women are oppressed by Islam

As the hair flows so
the woman goes.

—MUSLIM PROVERB

Zahra is a Tunisian woman who works at an engineering firm in New-port Beach, California. She is respected at her place of employment and feels at ease going to lunch with her colleagues, most of whom are male. Zahra is also a practicing Muslim, so she wears a head scarf, not out of obligation to her husband but because she is a spiritual woman and doesn't want her femininity to be a stumbling block in relating to men in public. Her decision to wear a scarf is as natural as putting on her work clothes each day. She doesn't feel oppressed wearing the scarf, but rather she feels empowered by it. Like many Muslim women, she is glad that her public persona will never be measured by her appearance. "I wear a head scarf in America because I can, I have the right to," says Zahra confidently. "The American Constitution entitles me to the right of freedom of worship. Where I am from, back in Tunisia, it was against the law for my mother to do so."

A Cover-Up?

But don't women suffer under Islam, you ask, and aren't they treated unfairly? Yes and no. No more than women throughout the centuries who have suffered a plethora of injustices because of antiquated social customs, superstitions, and religious bigotry. The oppression of women is not uncommon among the world's religions. "Sidelining women is not unique to Islam. Hindus, Buddhists, Jews, Christians and Muslims all have pigeonholed and stereotyped women at times," writes Miriam Adeney, author of *Daughters of Islam*. For centuries women have been seen as defective, the weaker sex, and lacking in the intellectual power of men. Given this tendency in religion, writes Adeney, it should not come as a surprise that many Muslims still hold this view.[1]

It has only been in the last century that Western women have won the right to vote and exercise control over their bodies through birth control. How can we expect much more from Third World countries that, in many respects, are on the cusp of technological and scientific revolutions?

Perhaps you suspect, like most Westerners, that Muslim women living in the West cover themselves in public out of obligation or that they will be severely punished by their fathers or husbands if they do not do so. At times you may look upon them with pity or even anger, as I have. Why don't they rise up and exercise their rights in the West?

> Anorexia, teenage pregnancy, sexually transmitted diseases, abortions, breast implants gone awry—these are seen as the consequences of a sexually loose society, of which devout Muslim women would rather have no part.

Oppression may be the reason why some women cover themselves, but many Muslim women living in the West cover themselves because they want to. Like Zahra, they take pride in their Muslim heritage and in their rich cultural traditions. In fact, some look down on Western women who dress sensually. They believe these women are enslaved as sexual objects in this society. Anorexia, teenage pregnancy, sexually transmitted diseases, abortions, breast implants gone awry—these are seen as the consequences of a sexually loose society, of which devout Muslim women would rather have no part.

In the late 1990s, several women who are celebrities in the United States focused the spotlight on the plight of Muslim women and raised questions about their freedoms and sense of fulfillment in life. Frightening images appeared on our televisions of poor, illiterate, and abused Afghani women shrouded in haunting, black veils. Yes, it's true that in some Islamic countries women are viewed with suspicion. They are believed to have little control over their sexual appetites, requiring men to control them to maintain societal order. Although in some places, such as Iran and the United Arab Emirates, women are punished, even tortured, for immodesty or sexual crimes, circumstances are very different for most Muslims living in the West.

Women who choose to cover themselves in the West do so usually because they have been raised by deeply religious parents. Single women wear head scarves to maintain family honor and in the hope of one day marrying a practicing Muslim man. Married women cover themselves because of family tradition, out of respect to their husbands, to be a good example to their children, and oftentimes because they feel more comfortable in public doing so. For them the head scarf or veil is a shield against unwanted attention from the world and from men in particular.

Modesty in a Modern World

Like a tightrope artist, a Muslim woman in the West carefully maneuvers through life, avoiding falling headlong into either Islamic fundamentalism or Western secularism. Either one would be the death of her feminine soul.

Outwardly, a Muslim woman must convey that she is intelligent, equipped to take on the challenges of the world, and modestly attractive. Her attractiveness, however, must be sophisticated in nature, never seductive. She does not buy into the theme often put forth in American advertising campaigns that to be powerful, one must also be sexy. Her femininity must be apparent but never used as a weapon or a tool in the workplace or in the public arena.

Like a tightrope artist, a Muslim woman in the West carefully maneuvers through life, avoiding falling headlong into either Islamic fundamentalism or Western secularism. Either one would be the death of her feminine soul.

To draw too much attention to her body, as women often do in Western entertainment and advertising, would be considered flirtatious or lewd. No cleavage, no bare tummies, no tight pants, and no short skirts. To dress provocatively would be disrespectful toward parents who believe it's their role to keep daughters chaste and focused on their studies and family life.

It's particularly challenging for adolescents and young adult Muslim women who want so much to fit in with their American or European peers. They see what women wear on TV and in the fashion magazines and they want to emulate them. Muslim girls know they stick out with their Eastern features and coloring. They hope their clothing will make them look more Western. Identifying too much with their non-Muslim peers, however, can raise a father's blood pressure. In some cases, fathers become so infuriated that they threaten to send their "wayward" girls back to their homeland, where they can be raised properly by grandmothers and aunts without the temptations and confusing messages of Western pop culture.

Growing Up with a Muslim Father

As the daughter of an Iranian father and an American mother, I learned about Muslim modesty the hard way. Having lost my mother to cancer just as I was entering puberty, I had little instruction about how to care for my changing appearance. My mother and I didn't have time to talk about the expectations my father would have for me to look modest as a young woman. I had to learn things by trial and error.

As an adolescent, I was creative and wanted to dress in a way that showed I was unique and daring. So I experimented with clothing and makeup, which did not delight my father when he saw some of my creations: red tights, polka-dotted short skirts, tie-dyed jeans, and dark eyeliner. I was ignorant of my father's ideals and never intentionally tried to infuriate him. As a Muslim man, he perceived that I was drawing too much attention to myself and looked promiscuous.

So he would do what came naturally to him as a Muslim parent. He'd reprimand me for my choices. "Take that eye makeup off right now!" "You're not wearing those clothes in public."

I felt confused, wounded. My American friends' parents didn't scold their girls for what they wore. Why did my dad? I needed help understanding my Muslim father's point of view.

My Eyes Were Opened

In my early twenties, I had a chance to travel to the Middle East and learn about Muslim modesty. Through personal observations and many conversations with Muslim women, I learned that the idea of modesty for Muslims is not only equated with sexual prudery but also is a matter of paying careful attention to one's outward appearance so as to never provoke a man to temptation through one's actions or dress. Most important, modesty protects women and family honor and is considered the same as godliness.

I was intrigued to learn that Muslim women are often savvy about sex, even if they do not appear to be so in public. From early childhood, Muslim girls are included in the grown-up discussions of the women of the family—mothers, grandmothers, aunts, cousins—about married life. A young bride, as she prepares herself for the act of lovemaking on her wedding night, is showered with grooming attention and advice from the married women in her family.

Since the sexual revolution of the 1960s and the widespread availability of birth control, sexual limitations and taboos in the West have, for many, been lifted. This openness about female sexual behavior, however, bewilders devout Muslims. It threatens the very fabric of their families and the dreams they have for their children's future. Parents ask, "How do we raise kids to be good Muslims and still fit in with their friends?"

These Muslims, along with devout Christians, believe that sex is sacred and a gift to be shared by a man and a woman in marriage. Keeping to that belief, however, is complex for Muslims living in the West. Their support structure here is small, while opposing messages are loud. At home, Muslim youth hear one thing; at school and on the streets they hear another.

No Dating

If Muslims feel this way about personal purity, what do they believe about the practice of dating? Derek, a junior at El Toro High School, has shown an interest in Fatima, a daughter of Arab immigrant parents. He regularly stops by her locker, makes small talk, and finally asks for her phone number. The problem is that Fatima's parents look down on dating.

Fatima doesn't want to discourage Derek's interest, but she tells him that her parents are very strict and don't allow her to see guys outside of school. Derek shakes his head in bewilderment and eventually turns his interest toward other girls on campus. Fatima is brokenhearted. She feels trapped by her parents' high standards but would never challenge her Muslim upbringing.

Muslims are taught from early childhood that they should not date as Westerners do. Dating is not a part of Muslim culture. Rather, courtship is reserved for engaged couples. And one's virginity is guarded for the marriage bed. Most Muslim families raise their sons and daughters to remain chaste. In some instances, a double standard exists: Muslim men who are known to be sexually active are not punished, whereas women are held to the stricter standard. However, most families do not openly support such behavior.

One night, at a dinner party, I met three medical students from Lebanon. The discussion turned to dating, and the three men unabashedly said they were virgins and planned to remain so until marriage. I marveled at their pride, knowing that most Western men would feel the opposite.

While I was growing up, my father and I never had talks about dating or sex—until my senior year of high school. Then things changed. Some classmates set me up on a blind date for a homecoming dance with a freshman in college. Naturally I was delighted and accepted the offer. I was permitted to attend the dance, but my father didn't like that the guy afterward had the nerve to call me regularly at home.

"What's he thinking?" my dad would ask me, with a stern expression on his face. "Why doesn't he come to the house and meet me? We should sit down and have a talk, man to man. I don't want him sneaking around trying to see you. That's disrespectful. And what about his parents? I should meet them too, you know."

No, I didn't know. I didn't know the first thing about my father's Muslim customs regarding dating and courtship. Living in Seattle, I had no Iranian grandmothers and aunts inviting me into their secret female world where I could have learned about men, courtship, and sex.

Like many Muslim youth in the West, I received my education on the customs of dating in a hit-or-miss fashion. I did something wrong and my father reacted. And then I would figure things out and move forward according to his wishes. Lucky for him, I was a compliant child—not perfect, but I figured out how to keep him happy most of the time.

In time I learned. It helped that I became a committed Christian in college. My father was open-minded; after all, he had married a Catholic in the '60s and didn't mind my involvement with a Christian group on campus. He didn't understand my eagerness to go to Bible study on campus and on short-term mission projects, but he was happy that I had friends who had good morals and would help keep me chaste. But not for the rest of my life, I later learned.

The summer after my freshman year in college, my father asked me in all sincerity if I planned on becoming a nun because I had become so active in Christian activities. Again I learned how different our worlds were. "No, Dad," I replied, trying not to smile. "I just found a great group of friends and hope I'm making a difference in the world. I'm not going to become a nun. I'm just living out my faith, that's all."

He looked relieved. "Well, when you're ready . . . let me know and I can help." He meant that he would help me find a husband.

Muslims and Matchmaking

So how does a Muslim find a mate? I wondered as I began to travel and come in contact with more Middle Easterners. I should have just asked my father, but I honestly didn't think about such things until I had the chance to live in Turkey as an exchange student. After my senior year at the University of Washington, I moved to Istanbul for a year with a small group of Americans. I was one of three women living together in an apartment near Bosphorus University. We were instructed by our American adviser to never spend time alone with men or invite them into our apartment unless it was for a large group social. We could go out in small groups of students or meet at a married couple's home. That's how proper Turkish women did things, and that was what was recommended for us in order to avoid problems with our neighbors and, potentially, with the authorities.

At first I thought the rules sounded archaic. I figured I could make some adjustments in my favor. I met with my friends and often stayed out late, not thinking how my neighbors might perceive me. Then one day a Turkish friend told me she had gotten an earful from the elderly Turkish man who lived above my apartment. He stopped her one day and proceeded to tell her how immoral we as American women were because we stayed out late at night and were never chaperoned. I couldn't believe the conclusions he had jumped to. Until then, I didn't realize how he interpreted our actions and schedule.

I wanted to please my neighbors and successfully finish out my year in Turkey. So I made the appropriate changes, limiting my time with friends to the daylight hours and never inviting men to our home unless a married couple or older adults were around. At first it wasn't easy to conform to such rigid rules, but I eventually adapted and still had a great year overseas.

When it comes to dating, I learned a woman must wait for relationships to come to her and oftentimes accept her parents' role in helping her choose a life partner. Arranged marriages are highly valued. Muslims are aware of the fact that, statistically, marriages for love end in divorce at a much higher rate than do arranged marriages. Many Muslims believe that arranged marriages benefit the whole family and often lead to a more secure and fulfilling marriage over the long term. When the marriage comes under strain, the couple has the support and counsel of both families.

A Muslim woman in the West is under some of the same restrictions when it comes to finding a husband. Dating usually is not an option. It's assumed that when the time is right, the man that a woman is interested in will approach her parents respectfully and ask for her hand in marriage. They are then engaged and begin the courtship, or the dating period, as we would call it in the West. A man and a woman can finally see each other privately with their parents' blessing while they prepare for marriage six to twelve months later. However, no sex. Both the man and the woman are to remain virgins, just in case the engagement is broken.

The Separation of Men and Women

Many Muslims are confused about the way men and women relate in the West. A lot of what we do and take for granted appears sexually immoral in their eyes. We raise our girls and boys to go to school together, play together, and date as early as junior high. Christian men and women sit together at church, pray out loud together, and in some cases a man and a woman will meet privately for counseling or Bible discussions. This kind of behavior is unheard of in Muslim countries, where men and women are always separated when it comes to religious activities so as not to distract one another.

Westerners need to understand that how we act toward one another in friendship and as coworkers may not be acceptable to a Muslim. When interacting with a Muslim, certain rules apply. A woman should not act too warmly toward a Muslim man on campus or in the work-place. Avoid eye contact and smiling at Muslim men unless you have been formally introduced or need to work together on a specific project. Even then your behavior should be professional, with little or no body contact. Never greet men with a hug or with too much enthusiasm. Such behavior is considered flirtatious and sexual in nature. The same rules apply for men greeting Muslim women.

Unfortunately, because of Western media and advertising, most Muslims do not realize that many Christians value sexual purity. They think we live no differently than Hollywood personalities they have read about who are living together and having children together without the legality of marriage. While I was dating my husband, a Muslim friend told me that she assumed Clyde and I were sleeping together. Because she believed that Christians were less moral than Muslims, she was surprised to find out we were not. I explained to her that sincere believers in Christ follow the Bible's instruction to be holy and therefore wait until marriage just as Muslims do. She was very pleased and inquired more about my faith.

Permission to Marry

Some of the scenes in the romantic comedy My Big Fat Greek Wedding remind me of the jolt my husband, Clyde, experienced when he called my father and asked for his permission to marry me. At the time, Clyde and I were working together in Colorado. Clyde wanted to surprise me with a romantic dinner and an engagement ring. The night before, he decided to call my father, who was living in California, to get his blessing. Clyde was not prepared for my father's response.

At first, Clyde very graciously made small talk with my father, whom he knew appreciated such pleasantries. Then he expressed his love for me and asked my father for my hand in marriage.

My father cleared his throat and told him what any well-meaning Muslim father would have said. "Clyde . . . (a long pause) I know you're a respectable young man. Shirin has spoken highly of you . . . (another long pause) but we have customs in my country that go back thousands of years. And marriage is not something we can talk about over the phone. So when you're ready to visit me in L.A., I'd be very happy to talk with you further about such an important matter."

"Uh . . . okay, Mr. Madani," Clyde said, his voice cracking. "How about this weekend? Could we fly out then and talk with you some more?"

"Certainly. I'd be very happy to introduce you to the family," my father replied warmly.

My husband's roommate later told me that Clyde turned white and fell over in his chair as he saw his plans destroyed. He was devastated.

Clyde called me at midnight and announced that we had to fly to Los Angeles over the weekend to talk to my father. "Why didn't you warn me?" he asked.

"I didn't know you'd propose so soon," I shot back.

Little did I know that Clyde had a diamond ring burning a hole in his pocket as we flew to L.A. on the red-eye and did the rounds of visiting all my Iranian relatives over the weekend. There were breakfasts and lunches and dinners to attend. He had to meet everyone, including my dying grandfather in the hospital. I knew things were going well when my father introduced Clyde to everyone as the "*dahmad*," which means "son-in-law" in Persian. But I didn't say anything to Clyde. I just let him enter into the experience.

I was proud of my heritage and the hoops that Clyde had to jump through to prove his love for me. Call me a romantic or old-fashioned, but I wouldn't want it any other way for my two daughters. Honestly, I think I will be even harder on them than my father was with me.

Living with High Standards

Remember Zahra, the engineer in Newport Beach who said she wears a head scarf not out of obligation to her husband but to honor him? She explained that in America she has the right to wear a scarf. It's important for Westerners to realize that not all Muslim women in the West wear head scarves out of obligation. Unfortunately, circumstances have changed for Zahra and she no longer covers her head. Her husband, the very man she desires to honor with her modesty, has asked her to no longer wear a scarf at work. It now worries him that her appearance may draw negative attention or even possible injury.

Parents and educators can learn much from the way Muslims raise their children to maintain high moral standards. At the same time we must be sympathetic to the unique challenges and tensions facing Muslims in the West, living in our secular society. As Christians, we can offer them our support and point to the strength and hope of Christ in raising godly families.

QUESTIONS FOR REFLECTION AND DISCUSSION

1. As you reflect on the story of Zahra, what do you admire most about her?

2. What elements of Muslims' views of modesty and sexual purity do you agree with? What can we learn from them?

3. What positive things do Christians and Muslims share in common in their views of sexuality and honoring parents?

all Muslims are radical fundamentalists

What distinguishes Islam, politi-
cally, from Christianity, is not that
one is more progressive or more
reactionary than the other, but
that Islam makes larger claims.

—EDWARD MORTIMER, *FAITH AND POWER*

Mustafa and Sibelle and their two children, Dursun and Mullud, live in
Seattle, Washington, as a Turkish immigrant couple. Mustafa moved to
the United States as a student in the late 1980s and then married and
sent for Sibelle, who is five years his junior. Two years later, they had
twin boys. They live in a four-bedroom home near Lake Washington;
their boys attend a public elementary school and play soccer and base-
ball through the local YMCA. They look like most American families:
two cars in the garage, a basketball hoop in the driveway, a barbecue in
the backyard, and a PlayStation in the recreation room for their sons to
enjoy with the neighborhood kids.

Yet they are secular Muslims. Sibelle dresses like most moms on her
block and even dons a pair of shorts in the summer. Mustafa fasts during the month of Ramadan but also enjoys a glass of wine once in a
while with dinner.

Muslims, says Mustafa, look to Islam as the foundation on which to build their lives. "We're all the same, but we're all different. Islam is a lifestyle. Muslim families in the West look different than families living in the Middle East. Living out my religion means living in peace. I do it the best I can here in the U.S."

Another couple, Muhammed and Khatija, are orthodox Muslims from Kuwait who, with the help of relatives, immigrated to the United States after the Gulf War in 1992. They and their five children live in a suburb of Chicago. Muhammed owns a dry-cleaning business, and Khatija teaches at her children's Muslim school. They live a quiet life, cultivating a vegetable and herb garden in their backyard, and rarely mingle with their neighbors. Khatija and her oldest daughter wear head scarves, and Muhammed attends a mosque with his teenage sons on Fridays at lunch. The family prides themselves on strong academics, financial security, and modest living.

For couples like Mustafa and Sibelle and Muhammed and Khatija, September 11 ushered in a new reality—the struggle between radical Islam and the West. Suddenly all Muslims seem like the enemy, willing to violently oppose our modern world. In the onslaught of negative media coverage, Muslims are often seen as a homogeneous group, unified in their intent to conquer the West and to change its culture through mass terror. This makes it increasingly difficult to engage in meaningful dialogue with Muslims about their worldview or issues related to events in the Middle East.

> In the onslaught of negative media coverage, Muslims are often seen as a homogeneous group, unified in their intent to conquer the West and to change its culture through mass terror. This makes it increasingly difficult to engage in meaningful dialogue with Muslims about their worldview or issues related to events in the Middle East.

But not all Muslims have the same religious orientation. Muslims are as diverse in religious practices, appearance, and lifestyle as are Christians. We take for granted that Christians in the West differ widely in their customs, dress, musical tastes, and views on using alcohol. Christians also disagree on some points of theology, such as the nature of the sacraments, the role of the Holy Spirit, the events surrounding Christ's return, and the inerrancy of the Bible. For the most part, in modern times, Christians accept the fact that differing points of view are manifested in different denominations and churches in the United States and around the world. Whether one is Episcopal or Greek Orthodox, Baptist or Roman Catholic, Missouri Synod Lutheran or Charismatic, we've learned to accept our differences and live in a neighborly manner.

> We take for granted that Christians in the West differ widely in their customs, dress, musical tastes, and views on using alcohol. Christians also disagree on some points of theology, such as the nature of the sacraments, the role of the Holy Spirit, the events surrounding Christ's return, and the inerrancy of the Bible.

Too often, Westerners fail to understand and appreciate the diversity of views and religious practices among Muslims. I've experienced some of this stereotyping when I tell people about my Middle Eastern background. Eyebrows raise and body language conveys suspicion or apprehension. I prepare myself for the expected question: "Does that mean your family is Muslim?"

"Yes, they are," I reply.

"Wow, that must be hard," they say with a look of pity in their eyes.

Yes and no. I understand that my American peers often assume the worst because of what they have heard about Islam. And I'm touched by their compassion. It's not easy being raised in a home with two different religions. But not all Muslims are the same, and my experience among Muslims has been mainly positive.

Diversity within Islam

Muslims, writes Edward Mortimer, author of *Faith and Power: The Politics of Islam*, are just as divided about the issues of politics, economics, and religion as any other group:

> In any given Muslim society and at any given time there is always more than one political interpretation of Islam being put forward.

Even if in many places, traditionalists' interpretations are now dominant, they are certainly not unchallenged. Nor is there in any country an effective consensus on what the authentic Islamic tradition consists of, or how much of it can be restored in practices, or how fast, or in what order.... Although many Muslims assert Islam is a complete system, not only ethically and religiously, but political, social and economic, clearly distinct from both socialism and capitalism, they are by no means in agreement.... Some see it as essentially democratic, while others argue that democracy is a Western notion that has nothing to do with Islam.[1]

Mind-boggling? So where do I start? you ask. How do I approach a Muslim colleague without offending him if I don't know what kind of Muslim he or she is?

Focus on points of commonality, even though finding common ground with Muslims may seem elusive because of the different languages, different traditions, different worldviews. Yet as we seek to gain understanding of the unfamiliar beliefs of Muslims, "different" can be less intimidating when we discover how much we are alike in our quest for happiness and meaning in life.

Whether they are Shiite or Sunni, you'll find a range of Muslims living in the West, everything from secular to radical fundamentalist. Learning to identify the types of Muslims in your sphere of relationships will help you to initiate more respectful dialogue and create more satisfying friendships. Let's take a minute to learn about the four types of Muslims living in the West. The Muslim in your circle of relationships may fit in one of the categories described below or may be a combination of two different groups.

> Whether they are Shiite or Sunni, you'll find a range of Muslims living in the West, everything from secular to radical fundamentalist. Learning to identify the types of Muslims in your sphere of relationships will help you to initiate more respectful dialogue and create more satisfying friendships.

Which Kind of Muslim?

Kamron seems modern enough. He wears a white polo shirt with blue jeans and drives a pickup. He talks freely with women in his classes, totes a backpack on campus, and carries a cell phone on his hip. You know he's a Muslim, and you wonder if he's a fundamentalist or in any way sympathetic to the recent Muslim-backed terrorism in the world. Kamron wonders if you see him as a terrorist or at least as sympathetic to their views. He hopes you'll make an effort to get to know who he really is.

Don't be afraid to ask your Muslim friend what kind of a Muslim he is. It may take him a minute to reply, because he's rarely asked about his faith. Most Muslims simply see themselves as Muslims. Most are Sunni Muslims, who believe the true line of succession from Muhammad is found in the four succeeding caliphs: Abu Bakr, Omar, Uthman, and Ali and their heirs. The rest are primarily Shiites, who believe that only Muhammad's son-in-law Ali, the fourth caliph, and his heirs are the true successors of Islam. (The reign of the caliphs ended in the 1920s after the First World War.) Other than being from the Shiite or Sunni branches, they don't think of themselves denominationally as Christians do. "I'm Southern Baptist," we remark nonchalantly. Or, "I'm Presbyterian, part of the P.C.U.S.A."

Most Muslims in the West, whether Sunni or Shiite, fall in the secular or moderate groupings. They simply either keep the law, pray, and fast, or they don't. They view their spiritual lives as private and don't openly talk about their religious practices the way Christians do. "I go to Bible study on Thursday mornings," says Sally. Or, "I read my Bible every morning before I go to work," Mark offers.

Many Muslims don't measure their spirituality by the number of times they read the Koran each week or how often they go to the mosque. I learned this while living in Istanbul, Turkey, as an exchange student. Although I did not speak to Muslim men in public, I would ask Muslim women about their spiritual lives and practices: Do you go to the mosque each week? Do you pray every day? Do you fast? Do you read the Koran regularly? Most did not. Yes, they believed, prayed from time to time, and participated in religious holidays, but most, both men and women, simply had inherited their family's religion. Very few Muslims in the West, in fact, are members of a mosque. Weddings and funerals usually are performed by a Muslim cleric in a rented hall or private home.

Radical Fundamentalists

The radical fundamentalist Muslim, the most visible to Westerners and the most troubling, is not only highly involved in his religion but also adamantly opposed to Western political and cultural beliefs, which he believes are guided by greed. The radical fundamentalist believes that Islam is superior to all other religions and is, therefore, in direct opposition to the West. His political aspirations are to build a society in which Islamic law prevails. He does not hide his sense of injustice and openly condemns America as the "Great Satan." He is usually bearded, keeps his veiled wife indoors, and is distant toward Westerners.

> The radical fundamentalist believes that Islam is superior to all other religions and is, therefore, in direct opposition to the West. His political aspirations are to build a society in which Islamic law prevails.

Radical fundamentalist Muslims are the small minority you see on the evening news and on the covers of news magazines such as U.S. News and World Report, beating their chests, burning flags, and cursing the leaders of the West. They support the tactics of Osama bin Laden and the Hezbollah, a Lebanese militant group trying to promote Islamic fundamentalism by force. They publish materials on their ideology and create websites to proselytize and to garner financial support for their cause. Yale University Islam expert Mary Habeck explains some of the fury behind their attacks: "They argue that it is the rest of the Muslim world that has fallen away—'apostatized'—and must be called back to the true way of life. . . . Bin Laden also hoped that the [9-11] attack would make clear to Muslims that the infidels were not invulnerable and . . . [that Muslims'] true religious duty lay in the jihad and the path of God with him."[2]

Though still a small minority, radical fundamentalists are backed by oil-rich sheiks and by some Muslim charities in the West. They are international students, businessmen, clerics, and fathers. Representing only 10 to 15 percent of Muslims worldwide, these radical fundamentalists are viewed by mainstream Muslims as a disturbing faction, far from the peace-loving identity so many Muslims prefer.

Secular Muslims

At the opposite end of Islam are the secular Muslims, nominal believers, perhaps even agnostics. They know very little about their religion, the Koran, or Muslim traditions. They may be a first-generation American or Canadian. Or a Turkish or Lebanese immigrant, known for being more moderate in their views about religion.

Secular Muslims live life very much the same as secular Westerners or Christians. Nothing about their manner or appearance communicates a pious life or interest in spiritual disciplines. The secular Muslim man may enjoy a beer during a football game, practice casual dating and premarital sex, pay interest on his credit cards (forbidden under Islamic law), be pro-choice, support the gay-rights movement, and marry a Westerner or a Christian. He may even allow his children to attend church with their Christian mother or with friends from school. The secular Muslim woman lives in much the same way as the Muslim man.

> Secular Muslims live life very much the same as secular Westerners or Christians. Nothing about their manner or appearance communicates a pious life or interest in spiritual disciplines.

They may be Democrat or Republican, a member of the NRA or the Green Peace movement. They could live in Santa Ana, California, or Topeka, Kansas. Nothing about them communicates that they are Muslim by birth. And they are perfectly happy about that.

Secular Muslims, for the most part, feel a mixture of shame and confusion as a result of the terrorist attacks on American soil. Some don't understand Muslim hostility toward the West or why more Islamic nations aren't democracies. A number of these secular Muslims living in the United States are patriotic and support the U.S. government's war against terrorism.

Secular Muslims are open to discussion about a variety of topics in life: current events, the arts, sports, politics, philosophy, and religion. They may regret that they don't know more about their country of origin or their religion. They may even openly question the tenets of Islam but still feel a strong attachment to their heritage.

Moderate Muslims

Moderate Muslims practice their faith by praying up to five times a day or as often as they can fit it into their schedule; they read the Koran occasionally, fast during the month of Ramadan, and hope to visit Mecca someday on a pilgrimage. A moderate Muslim man is not, however, likely to visit a mosque regularly. A moderate Muslim woman will not wear a head scarf or dress conservatively. And a moderate Muslim man may occasionally drink alcohol or wear a necktie. Some marry Christians.

As the moderate Muslim man begins to identify more with his religious heritage, he may ask his Christian fiancée or wife to convert to Islam for the sake of their future children and to protect family harmony. He may become more outwardly religious later in life or after the death of a loved one.

Moderate Muslims often enjoy friendships with both Muslims and non-Muslims. They move about easily in life in the West. Many have strong ties back home and may travel there to visit relatives every couple of years. They often are successful in the workplace and in their relationships because they are mild-mannered, have self-control, and are generous, tolerant, and open spiritually.

Moderate Muslims are troubled by the strain between the West and the Muslim world. They often feel a deep allegiance to both sides of the conflict. They worry that leaders in the West may underestimate the incredible challenge of bringing harmony and freedom to war-torn countries like Afghanistan and Iraq. In many respects, they'd prefer for the United States to keep out of the Middle East.

When it comes to raising a family, moderate Muslim parents often feel torn regarding the education and lifestyle of their children living in the West. They want their children to have friends and to fit in with their peers, but they fear that the tide of sexual immorality and materialism will pull their children's hearts far from home. They desire for their children to live modest, godly lives. They want their children to succeed in school and rise to positions of leadership in society.

Muslim men and women enjoy discussing topics with Christians related to theology and spiritual discipline and recognize that in many respects they have more in common with practicing Christians than they do with secular members of Western society.

Orthodox Muslims

Orthodox Muslims are the most noticeably Muslim-looking individuals in the West. Easily identifiable by their clothing and mannerisms, they are well schooled about their faith and Islamic traditions. They usually are highly involved in their local mosque and may enroll their children in Muslim schools. They often buy their groceries from an Islamic market and prefer to not eat with non-Muslims, fearing that the food may not have been prepared in a clean manner. They keep to their own social circles and vigilantly guard their children's innocence.

Orthodox Muslim women wear a head scarf or veil. They avoid contact with men in public and socializing with strangers. They are modest, submissive, and outwardly quiet. Married women pride themselves on being hospitable and in preparing meals, which sometimes is an all-day affair. They are excellent housekeepers, good with children, and usually have strong ties to their homeland.

Married Orthodox Muslim women often shop with one another and gather for afternoon tea or join a women's group at a mosque. They read to their children from the Koran and prepare their daughters for a life of marriage and child-rearing. Many are bilingual and have graduated from a university. They are curious about the family life of Westerners.

Orthodox Muslim men often have a beard and avoid the Western custom of wearing ties. They are the spiritual head of their family and may lead the family in prayer or in reading the Koran. They attend the mosque on Fridays at noon, which also serves as their social circle and avenue for news from back home.

An orthodox Muslim father prides himself in his ability to provide for his family. He takes pride in having a faithful wife and children with proper social etiquette, good grades, and respect for elders. He is likely to prefer that his family remain anonymous, isolated from Western life, living quietly while preserving Islamic culture and traditions at home.

He frowns on the Western notion of dating and premarital sex. He prefers to assist his children in matchmaking and is an advocate of arranged marriage. He enjoys socializing over a game of backgammon or a glass of tea, mainly with friends who share his nationality and religion. He is uncomfortable with friendly Western women, especially those in positions of leadership in the workplace.

He prefers to keep an arm's-length away from Christians who evangelize and avoids openly Christian celebrations or public events. He may be critical of America's involvement in the Middle East and in the Israeli-Palestinian conflict, and bitter about the war in Iraq. However, he does not pose a threat to national security and is committed to living a quiet, private life.

A Day in the Life of . . .

To spend time with a Muslim is to open your eyes to the world, to experience the rich diversity of God's creation, to get in touch with ancient cultures that in many respects are more similar to the customs of Jesus of Nazareth than to our customs. To spend time with a Muslim woman is to learn to appreciate the art of hospitality and modest beauty as well as her undying commitment to family and friends. To spend time with a Muslim man is to learn to appreciate loyalty to forefathers and to enjoy the art of storytelling or a good soccer match or to savor afternoon tea. Muslims are some of the warmest and most hospitable people I know.

Like Christians, Muslims are hurt when a colleague or a friend makes assumptions about their religious beliefs, practices, or political views. An orthodox Muslim woman, for example, would be hurt to learn that her American neighbors view her as oppressed and unhappy in her marriage because she wears a head scarf. A secular or moderate Muslim would be embarrassed to be categorized with a fundamentalist. A number of Muslims in the United States are card-holding Republicans and support military deployment in the Middle East.

At times I hear Muslims spoken about in derogatory terms when I know that Americans generally know so little about their personal lives. Muslims are not all the same. Yet in many ways, Muslims have the same dreams as everyone else—dreams of a good life, success, freedom, and happiness.

Let these common aspirations provide a safe environment in which to get to know each other, to share our lives as friends.

In the next chapter, we'll begin to look at some ways we can build friendships with Muslims by understanding their view of relationships, hospitality, child-rearing, and work. As we learn to build bridges of friendship with Muslims in a welcoming and respectful manner, we can remove the barriers of cultural misunderstandings and begin to more graciously represent the love of Christ.

QUESTIONS FOR REFLECTION AND DISCUSSION

1. What kinds of Muslims live in your sphere of relationships—secular, moderate, orthodox, or radical fundamentalist? If you're not sure, how could you find out?

2. Have you asked your Muslim friends about their religious practices or beliefs? Why or why not? What hinders Christians in the West from learning about the religious beliefs and practices of Muslims?

3. How has the information in this chapter helped you to better understand Muslims at your workplace? What information about Muslims surprised you?

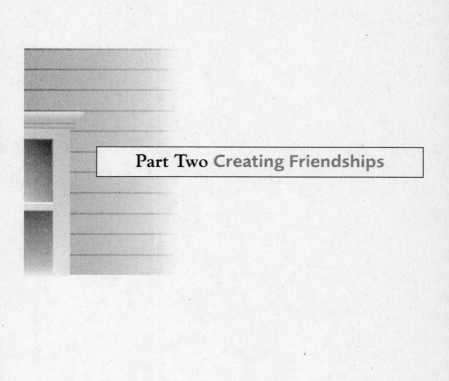

Part Two Creating Friendships

CHAPTER 7

entertaining, Muslim style

For most Muslims, friend-
ship involves an investment
of time and effort: to be
together, to relate to one
another, share food, talk
and much more.

—TOM PHILLIPS ET AL.,
THE WORLD AT YOUR DOOR

We are gently admonished in Hebrews 13:2 to "not forget to entertain strangers, for by so doing some people have entertained angels without knowing it."

Muslims believe the same about entertaining strangers and regularly quote similar proverbs from their own sacred writings. This belief has led to rich Muslim traditions and a great devotion to entertaining their guests. Whether it's an elaborate holiday meal or an impromptu afternoon tea, Muslims believe it's their duty to welcome their guests in a manner that communicates respect and appreciation. Nothing warms a Muslim's heart more than genuine hospitality.

When Westerners host Muslims in their home, there is great potential for joy, but just as much potential for disappointment. More often than not, Muslims are confused by a Westerner's notion of hospitality. In the hustle and bustle of our modern age, too many of us have lost sight of the art of hospitality. Let me tell you the story of Ferhad and his first trip to America—his hopes and disappointments, but most of all his cultural misunderstandings.

The Visiting Professor

Ferhad, a middle-aged economics professor at Istanbul University in Turkey, arrives at the airport in Los Angeles, delighted to finally be visiting America. He has been invited to attend an international conference for educators at UCLA. An American acquaintance in Istanbul arranged for him to stay with an American family near the campus. In love with American cinema and music, the trip—to visit the "capital" of entertainment—is a dream come true for Ferhad.

With a sparkling smile and a warm hug, Jeremy, a youth pastor, welcomes Ferhad at the airport. Loading Ferhad's luggage into the back of his black Ford Expedition, Jeremy freely makes conversation and praises Ferhad for his work as an educator. Jeremy's enthusiasm warms Ferhad's heart. He likes feeling respected and being told his work is worthwhile.

Speeding along the highway, Ferhad marvels at the California scenery: expensive cars, majestic palm trees, and luxury hotels. Ferhad can hardly believe his eyes—so much wealth and beauty in one land. He looks forward to some sightseeing and learning firsthand about the American culture.

Thirty minutes later, Jeremy pulls his vehicle into the driveway of his two-thousand-square-foot home in Long Beach and hurriedly escorts Ferhad into the house, apologizing that he has a meeting to attend before dinner. Inside, Ferhad is welcomed by three gregarious children under the age of seven and a tired, frazzled young mother. Jeremy's wife, Kris, shoos the children into the small backyard and joins them, reclining on a lawn chair with a diet Coke and magazine in hand. Jeremy leads Ferhad to his room, telling him to make himself at home and to grab anything from the fridge if he's hungry.

Ferhad looks at Jeremy wide-eyed, dumbstruck that he will be left alone with Jeremy's wife without so much as a cup of tea before Jeremy leaves. Hearing Jeremy's car pull out of the driveway, Ferhad collapses in an easy chair in the corner of his room. Tired from the long journey, feeling trapped inside an unfamiliar home and abandoned by his host, he questions the wisdom of his housing arrangement with an American family.

Ferhad remains in his room despite the grumbling of his stomach. Finally, his eyes become heavy and he falls asleep. Jeremy arrives home at 6:45, taps gently at Ferhad's door, and announces it's time for dinner. Groggy and a little disoriented, Ferhad shuffles to his feet, washes his face, applies some cologne, changes into a clean shirt, and arrives in the kitchen with a smile on his face. In his hand he carries a large, gift-wrapped hand-painted Oriental plate, which he presents to Kris, thanking her in advance for dinner. Kris blushes, unaccustomed to such formalities, and turns abruptly to hush the children, who are clanking their dinnerware on the table.

Ferhad stares questioningly at the kitchen table. *Dinner?* he asks himself. A large bowl of steaming beans and ground beef in a tomato sauce, a smaller bowl of grated orange cheese, a green salad with a few cherry tomatoes, and a basket of sliced white bread. Ferhad's stomach growls in disappointment and his spirits drop another notch.

Ferhad spends the next five days either on campus or at Jeremy's home, eating simple dinners in front of the TV. Meanwhile, Jeremy is busy running church meetings, leading Bible studies, and organizing youth activities.

Ferhad enjoys his conference and meeting other internationals, but he had hoped his trip would offer him much more. In the end, the only California sites Ferhad saw were those en route to his conference from Jeremy's home and to the airport for his flight home.

At the airport, Jeremy hugs Ferhad at the curb, wishes him safe travel back home, and says he hopes Ferhad had a good visit to the United States. Ferhad boards his plane, reclines his seat, and ponders his stay with an American family. What went wrong? Why was he so disappointed? How would things be different if Jeremy were to visit him in Turkey?

Closing his eyes, Ferhad imagines entertaining Jeremy in his own country. Ferhad's wife would prepare delicious meals fit for a king and serve them in the dining room. Afterward, they would retire to the living room to enjoy a platter of exotic fruits, pastries, several cups of hot tea, and pleasant conversation. A day of his time would be sacrificed to take Jeremy sightseeing, shopping at the covered bazaar, and dining at a fine restaurant on the waterfront. Ferhad would not be content until his guest had thoroughly enjoyed himself and had plenty of souvenirs and happy stories to take home with him.

Meeting Expectations

Jeremy and Ferhad have very different views of hospitality. Coming from the East, Ferhad clearly expected much more from his trip to the United States. He wanted to go sightseeing. He expected more elaborate meals, served in an atmosphere of relaxed hospitality. But like most Muslims, he did not speak about his desires. Rather, he hoped his host would have the foresight to meet his expectations.

Jeremy was unprepared to have a Muslim guest in his home. He graciously provided room and board but didn't make time in his schedule for much else. Like most Americans, he is busy and his time is filled with work and family activities. His intentions are good, but he had no idea how to properly entertain a Muslim.

Jeremy should have inquired about what would be expected of him and his family while hosting a Muslim in his home. He should have asked:

■ What foods should I serve?

■ How should I organize my schedule to best accommodate a Middle Easterner in my home for several days?

■ What topics of conversation should I initiate or avoid?

■ How can I show my guest he is valued and respected?

Americans are known for a casual attitude when it comes to entertaining. We are comfortable with hamburgers on the grill, an ice chest filled with sodas, a basket of potato chips, and brownies for dessert.

Our lifestyles are different and so are our customs. The traditions passed on to us by our parents are different from the traditions passed down to Muslims. Taking time to learn about other cultures and their customs can help us to properly prepare for guests and avoid disappointment and hurt feelings. Instead, just by doing a few simple things, like serving familiar foods or offering a gift, we can foster mutual respect and build deep and lasting friendships.

Here are a few things we can do to make our social interactions with one another more mutually satisfying.

Visiting a Muslim's Home

Here's what you can expect and what you should do when you are invited into a Muslim's home. Remember that the offering and accepting of food is a form of communication. In the first example, Jennifer has been invited to a neighbor's home for afternoon tea.

"I'm so pleased you've made time in your schedule to come visit me," says Shoreh, a Muslim housewife. She hands Jennifer a cup of tea and offers her a platter of cookies.

"Yes, I'm honored that you opened your home to me," replies Jennifer, an American neighbor. And she accepts the tea and some cookies.

When you are invited to a Muslim home for a meal, you will be treated like an honored guest. Several courses and a plethora of delicacies will be served in your honor.

Imagine that Shandiz and Mitra, a young couple from Iran, have invited you to their home for dinner. They both speak English fluently but are new to Western life and to entertaining non-Muslims in their home. They are eager to make American friends and are delighted that you've accepted their invitation. They hope that you will have them over in return sometime in the near future.

You arrive on time and are welcomed warmly into their home. Wisely, you bring the hostess a special gift, like a colorful bouquet of flowers, a pretty candy dish, or fragrant soaps for the bathroom. The gift communicates that you know your hostess has gone to great lengths to prepare for your special visit.

The first thing that strikes you when you enter Shandiz and Mitra's home are the smells—a combination of sweet and sour, garlic and saffron, dill and mint. Their home is nicely furnished, more elegant than other American homes you've visited in your neighborhood. Persian carpets, white leather couches, a crystal chandelier, a samovar in the corner, and expensive lace curtains hang from the windows. The coffee table is loaded with a platter of cookies, a fruit bowl, candy dishes, and a bowl of nuts. Tea or coffee is served immediately in fine china cups. Several main course dishes are on display on the dining room table, two to three times the amount most Westerners would prepare.

Prior to your visit, you've learned that guests show their love by sampling all the dishes. So you accept several helpings and thank the hostess for her hard work in preparing the meal. When you have eaten enough, according to Muslim custom you leave a little on your plate so that the hostess will not feel obliged to offer you more.

When it's your turn to invite Shandiz and Mitra to your home, make the first impression count. Your coffee table should have an abundance of pastries or party foods, such as cookies, nuts, fruit, and chips. Offer your guests several cups of tea or coffee, insisting they have another, since it is the Muslim custom to politely refuse the first offer of a refill. Always serve your guests first (a platter of cookies or seconds at the dinner table) before serving yourself. Lavish them with love. Make them feel like a king or queen.

Clothing Counts

It's important as a guest in a Muslim home to dress both tastefully and modestly. An American woman should avoid clothing that draws too much attention to her figure or shows too much skin. No shorts or mini-skirts. No cleavage-revealing blouses or tank tops. No sweats or athletic wear. Think business casual or evening wear, even during the day.

A man should wear slacks and a button-down shirt or sweater. No jeans and T-shirts, sweats, or shorts.

If you have teenage daughters, ask them to dress in a way that will not offend your Muslim guest or host. Perhaps rather than wearing a pair of shorts and a short T-shirt that leaves the midriff bare, they could don an attractive skirt and matching top, something they might wear to church or to an interview for an after-school job. Another hint: in the eyes of a Muslim, your children are a reflection of your standards and commitment to clean, decent living.

Events Take Priority

Unlike Westerners, many Muslims are "event-oriented" rather than "time-oriented." That means a special event or relationship has priority over time constraints. For example, it is considered rude to look at your watch repeatedly while visiting with a Muslim because it signals that you have another meeting or appointment. Many Muslims would rather be late for their next appointment than leave in a manner that appears hurried or disrespectful. This can be maddening for Westerners, who are exceedingly time conscious.

For Muslims, developing a relationship in business is just as important as making the deal. When conducting business over a meal or a cup of coffee with a Muslim, Westerners should try to communicate that their time together is not only important but enjoyable.

It's also helpful to know that Muslims are not as punctual as Westerners when it comes to social events. It's customary to be thirty minutes to an hour late. A Muslim woman, for example, may linger in a flower shop selecting just the right arrangement as a gift for the hostess even though that means she'll arrive late for dinner. A Muslim man may get tied up talking to overseas relatives on the phone and be late for a social engagement. Muslims will wait for their guests to arrive before eating dinner, even if it is as late as nine in the evening.

When relating to Muslims, you can avoid needless frustration by adding some extra time to your schedule. If invited for tea, plan to spend the entire afternoon together. When preparing dinner for your Muslim friends, plan your meal in such a way that the food will not be ruined if your guests arrive an hour or more late.

Most of all, Muslims are looking for friendship and will sense your genuine interest in them. Relax. Linger. Remember: nothing warms a Muslim's heart more than a welcoming atmosphere and preparations that show them you've gone out of your way in their honor. Make time for proper entertaining. Make every meal count. Dress respectfully. And when invited to a Muslim's home, don't forget a gift.

QUESTIONS FOR REFLECTION AND DISCUSSION

1. What suggestions in this chapter were most helpful to you?

2. If you haven't entertained a Muslim in your home yet, what apprehensions do you have? How can you overcome them?

3. If finding time to build friendships with Muslims is a problem, what could you do to make the time for some specific situations?

4. What are some examples of ways you or other people in your church or small group might entertain some Muslims in your area? Can you think of any creative ideas to demonstrate your hospitality?

Entertaining Muslims In Your Home

- Clean the kitchen and dining area of clutter before guests arrive.
- Set a table with your best dishes and cloth napkins.
- Serve appetizers with tea, juice, and soft drinks, and mingle before dinner.
- Seat husbands and wives together.
- Avoid serving alcohol.
- Prepare foods with a variety of colors and flavors.
- Avoid dishes with pork.
- Serve tea or coffee with dessert.

forging alliances through our families

> No church, community, or
> nation will rise higher than
> the spiritual condition of
> its families.
>
> —DENNIS RAINEY,
> *BUILDING STRONG FAMILIES*

"I was surprised to note that there are a lot of conservative Christians and Jews who are raising their children in the same way we do," writes Sahar El-Shafie, a social studies teacher at Martin Middle School in Raleigh, North Carolina.[1] Sahar, a Muslim, found that she has many things in common with her Methodist coworker. They both believe in a sovereign God. They both agree on prayer and the need to trust God with the details of life.

And you'll probably find, like Sahar, that you have more in common with Muslims than you realize when it comes to raising children. Our commonalties can help us forge friendships.

Muslims love children and have a high regard for an orderly home. Desiring to preserve their family traditions and their children's innocence, they often ponder whether to send their children to public schools or to Muslim schools. Some Muslims even consider homeschooling as an alternative to public schools or expensive private schools.

Sadly, many believe that the social and emotional problems their children face—materialism, atheism, sexual promiscuity, drug use, eating disorders, and racism—are directly related to certain aspects of Western culture.

Many want to preserve their family's Islamic identity but find it difficult to do because of isolation and lack of religious resources in the West. They either do not have access to a local mosque or they shy away from becoming members because of possible negative reactions from American neighbors or colleagues. Often they feel directionless and ambivalent about how to integrate their spiritual beliefs with their secular lives and how to create a home environment which fosters spiritual disciplines and righteous living. A great number of Muslim parents, Sahar writes, are so busy trying to make ends meet that they feel too tired at the end of the day to pray together or read the Koran.[2]

As Christians we have much to offer Muslims in the area of raising and educating children. Christians have a head start in homeschooling and are therefore well-equipped to help Muslims find co-ops, select curriculum, and organize play groups. The opportunities are infinite.

Having been raised in a Middle Eastern home in the United States and having Muslim friends here, I'm acquainted with how eager Muslims are to build alliances with American families. When I was growing up in Seattle, my Iranian father often looked to the examples of other American parents when it came to raising his children. At times he needed their help with issues related to after-school sports, dating, and the challenges of raising adolescents. When he was out of work, or when his second marriage suffered, he needed a listening ear, career advice, and the prayers of faithful Christians. The world is filled with parents just like my father.

How can we reach out to people like that? Are there ways we can assist a Muslim family in raising their children in a culture that is not their own?

Fariba is a single mother who calls me from time to time to ask if her son can come over to my house to play. She knows he's safe in my Christian home, away from the TV and violent computer games. She knows her son will play as children should: climbing trees, swimming at the pool, shooting baskets, and sharing a family meal at the dining room table. At the same time, I'm open with her about my spiritual beliefs and have invited her son to church.

By building a sense of community with like-minded Muslims in our neighborhoods and in our children's schools, we can work together to make our living situations a safe and pleasing environment for our families.

Making a Difference in the Baby Blues

Few things in life are more difficult than the loneliness of going through the arrival of your first child without support from family or friends. I know, I have been there. I had my first child two and a half months after my husband and I were stationed in Paris, France. I had no one to turn to for help, no one to bring me meals, no one to just hold the baby for a while when it was fussy, no one to give me advice. A book on parenting became my best friend and mentor. Thanks to that book, I learned to follow a schedule that brought harmony to my baby's days and nights. The rest of the time, I tried to busy myself at home, read as many books as I could, and work on learning French with a tutor. But nothing took away the deep feelings of isolation and inadequacy.

Looking back, I've come to realize that the ultimate benefit of my isolation experience was learning to feel what it's like to be in a foreigner's shoes—lonely and unsure where to find the answers to the basic questions of life in a culture that is different from your own: Which pediatrician should I go to? Why does my baby cry every night before dinner? Where can I find some friends, some other new mothers? How can I improve my foreign language skills and still be a stay-at-home mom? When will I ever feel normal again?

Today numerous Muslim couples living in the West are asking the same questions. Their loneliness and fears may even feel more severe because many were raised in tight-knit families in their homelands prior to immigrating to the United States or Canada.

Unlike most Muslim women, as an American I had learned to become independent at a relatively young age. I went to college away from home, arranged for my own financial aid, started my own savings account at the age of eighteen, and began traveling overseas by the end of my sophomore year.

Most Muslim girls are raised to be dependent on their families until marriage. They rely heavily on their parents for their education, social development, and finances. They grow up believing in the dream that one day when they have children, their mother and aunts and cousins will be nearby to help them, taking over all the day-to-day tasks so that they can concentrate on nursing and cuddling the baby. They are unprepared for the challenges of pregnancy and the exhausting routine of caring for a baby. They need a helping hand, friendship, and perhaps some coaching on the basics of child care. They need surrogate grandparents and uncles and aunts to give their children a chance to cultivate a respect for elders, which Muslims hold in high regard. They need meals brought to their home after the birth of a baby, books on parenting, a mothers' support group, a listening ear, and a night out once in a while with their husband. They need what all new parents need—good friends with some parenting experience.

Making a Difference in Educating Children

Muslim parents often pride themselves on the academic successes of their children. Like Asians living in the West, Muslims are demanding and push their children to work hard at their studies. And the results are usually very respectable. There is a lot of parental pressure to go to the right school and to pursue graduate studies. I respect my heritage and the goals my family has passed down to me. As a parent, I now find myself wanting my own children to perform with excellence in their education.

Not every Muslim family finds the path to educational success to be smooth and free of potholes. Majid, a forty-two-year-old Muslim father, enrolled his two adolescent children in a private school, hoping they'd learn to take school more seriously and prepare for a successful college experience. His English is limited, so he hoped the private school environment would ensure his children received more attention from the teachers and even tutoring if needed.

Six months later, much to his dismay, Majid's children continue to struggle with school, pulling in low B and C averages, and they are gravitating toward the wrong crowd. The hundreds of dollars Majid spends on tuition each month does not guarantee that teachers will make time to address his children's poor math and English scores or direct them toward a better peer group.

Majid feels anger and fear. Because of his limited English, he is unable to help his children with their homework. His wife works long hours at her job and has little reserve at the end of the day to tutor the kids. His closest relatives live an hour away. Where can he get help? How can he get his kids to perform better? He now wonders if his kids would be better off back in Iran, with its strict religious and political climate.

Majid's concerns are not unusual. Muslims often feel ill-equipped to handle the ups and downs of their children's education in a strange language and culture. Perhaps you have a Muslim neighbor or know a parent at a school or place of business who is experiencing some of the same struggles. Whether it's fear of bad grades, teacher-parent conflicts, or a curriculum that supports minors' using birth control or promotes homosexuality, the concerns are the same for both Muslim and Christian parents.

Sharing a similar vision for our children's education and social development can foster open and authentic conversations about spiritual beliefs and practices. Oftentimes Muslims recognize that devout Christians raise their children differently than secular parents and in a manner similar to their own ideals. Christian parents can then share how they turn to God for answers and guidance in promoting holy living among their youth. For those Muslims who struggle with isolation, being invited to visit a church or a Bible study group may bring some comfort and spiritual direction. But such matters require prayer and gentleness at all times on the part of the Christian, who seeks not to offend the Muslim parents or to oversimplify their problems and struggles with their children.

Making a Difference in Marriage and Divorce

Muslim couples living in the West are not immune to the troubles that plague marriages.

Amine and Sheida are friends of mine whose marriage is in trouble. They moved to Ontario, Canada, seventeen years ago, before having children. The early years were exciting, with the thrill of change. The possibilities for success seemed endless. But the demands of caring for their first child and the fear of being laid off changed their lives. Amine's heart began to wander. He started coming home late from work, having secretly turned to a coworker to have his needs met. Within a few weeks, Sheida suspected the worst, called her parents back home to tell them she was getting a divorce, packed Amine's bags, and threw them out on the driveway.

Amine pleaded and begged and won Sheida's heart back, promising never to cheat on her again. He sent her flowers, bought her perfume, and even offered to babysit Saturday afternoons so she could spend some time alone at the mall. Sheida let him back in the house and called her parents, telling them the divorce had been called off.

But six months later, Amine came home at one in the morning with lipstick on his shirt collar. Sheida flipped. She again packed his bags and threw them out on the driveway. But this time Amine piled his suitcases on the backseat of his Camry, drove off, and moved in with his new girlfriend.

Sheida wept bitterly for days, alarming her two-year-old son and her neighbors. Then she stopped and assessed her situation. Her ranting and raving, she finally told herself, hadn't produced anything positive. Instead, she now had a broken marriage and little chance for restoration.

In their homeland, their parents would have intervened to help the couple save their marriage. There also is more peer pressure to make a marriage last. But in Canada, Sheida and Amine had none of that and eventually had little reason to stay together.

During times of difficulty in a marriage, Muslim couples recognize they're truly alone living in the West. Divorce flattens them, leaving them more lonely than they've ever felt before, thousands of miles away from a supportive family and close friends.

My husband, Clyde, and I take the time to ask our Muslim friends how they're getting along in their marriage. We ask the wife how she is adjusting to life in the West. When our schedules permit, we offer to babysit so they can get some much needed time alone. We invite them into our home so they can see how we function as a family. When appropriate, we offer to pray for them. Sometimes this is after a quiet time of talking about their personal problems.

Making a Difference in Sickness and Death

It's not only child-rearing and marriage problems that can create opportunities to reach out to Muslims in our communities. Sickness and death also leave people needy. But it's important to recognize that other cultures deal with sickness and death differently. Some deal with it openly, even matter-of-factly. Others treat the subject delicately, even to the point of denial. I remember as a young teenager when my Iranian grandmother died and my American neighbor had to break the news to me. My grandmother had, in fact, died several weeks earlier, but my father didn't have the heart or the constitution to tell me.

It wasn't until I studied more about Muslim culture in college that I learned that sickness and death are both taboo subjects. Muslims feel uncomfortable talking openly about such matters. If, for example, a Muslim's relative dies while he was out of town or out of the country, it is likely that his family would avoid telling him until he returned home. The reasons are varied: they don't want to overwhelm, they don't want to frighten, they don't want to be the bearer of bad news.

The matter is complicated and should be handled sensitively by Westerners. If the subject of serious illness or death surfaces with your Muslim friends or fellow workers, ask regularly how they are doing. Show respect and gentleness when referring to the sick person or the deceased. Assume that the pain is ongoing for them. Offer to pray for the family. Send flowers or take a meal to the family's home. Dress appropriately in dark clothing for funerals and wakes. A Muslim wake is a very sad, solemn time. Women and men sit in different rooms and wail and cry out loud.

It's good to recognize that Muslims usually mourn for anywhere from forty days to a year. During the mourning period, they refrain from public displays of celebration, including weddings. Some Muslims will wear black for an entire year. They may seem melancholy for several months. Their attachments to the deceased are very strong. They may hang the deceased person's picture in the entryway of their home or on the living room mantel. They are hurt when Westerners expect them to move quickly through the mourning process. They need our patience, understanding, and Christian love demonstrated through acts of kindness.

Demonstrating Acceptance to Our Children

Children need strong role models in order to learn to develop a sense of acceptance and tolerance toward others. Demonstrating acceptance is the responsibility of all adults, especially parents, educators, and those in the ministry, and not something kids should have to figure out on their own.

Nicole came home from school one day and told her father, over a plate of cookies and a glass of milk, that a boy she knows, Omid, is a bad boy.

"Why do you say that?" her father asked.

"Because he's Muslim. And you know what those bad Muslim people did to New York City, right?"

"Well, has Omid done anything bad to you?"

"Um . . . no, not really."

"Does he act differently than the other boys in your class?"

"Uh, not exactly . . . but he's Muslim, Dad. You know what I mean?"

"No, I don't, honey. We have to be careful how we treat people who are a little different than we are. I'm sure Omid is a nice boy. If you're worried about him, I can talk to your teacher and see what she thinks."

"Oh, don't worry about it," Nicole said nonchalantly. She grabbed another cookie and ran upstairs to play with her little sister.

Nicole's father was wise to know that his child will model his thinking and reactions when it comes to dealing with people with a different background and from a different culture. We live in a time when you're likely to hear your child talk about the differences among people, especially (since 9-11) the differences between Christians and Muslims.

Whether you are a parent or not, each of us must deal with prejudices, our own and the prejudices of others. How we deal with them requires serious self-examination.

Making the effort to get to know these Muslim "strangers" in our land starts with a smile and a simple greeting—"Good morning," "Hello." Show an interest without being intrusive. When

> Each of us must deal with prejudices, our own and the prejudices of others. How we deal with them requires serious self-examination.

your children see you interacting with someone from a different part of the world, they learn how they too can become friends with the new kid in class. As you and a Muslim become better acquainted, you may want to invite the Muslim into your home so that your children can learn to feel comfortable around people of another culture. Books and videos are a good way to learn about other cultures.

Keep it simple and be as clear as you can when discussing prejudice and racism with your child. Be honest about tensions, but not to the point of creating fear in your child. Try to encourage your child to value friends from different cultures and social groups. Be careful not to make derogatory remarks. And don't overprotect. Help your children to pray for their friends and their enemies. Model God's love for all of his creation.

Unselfish Love

After my mother died of cancer, I experienced firsthand the unselfish love of the neighbors across the street. I told our story in the opening chapter of this book. The friendship between Pamela and my mother, two neighbors, had started months before. And after my mother died, Pamela and her husband unselfishly took in my brothers and me and helped to raise us. They didn't allow cultural barriers and prejudices to stand in the way of God's call to help the Muslim-Catholic family across the street that was so very different from their own.

Their unselfish love touched me deeply and serves as a personal motivation to do the same for others. God used Pamela to change my life. I was fourteen, an Iranian-American girl just trying to fit in, when I lost my mother to leukemia. My life would not be the same today without

Pamela's sacrifice and influence. Pamela, and others like her, mothered my two younger brothers and me and helped us navigate life's difficult waters. They saw us through not only the high school years but also college, marriage, and now into parenthood.

Like Pamela, countless others—parents of childhood friends, coaches, educators, laymen, and pastors—took time to befriend us, mentor us, and direct us toward successful and fulfilling lives. My brothers and I were lifted up and directed toward activities and goals that helped us to become proper citizens and, more important, followers of Christ. So what I write in these pages about getting to know your Muslim neighbor or coworker or fellow student is more than abstract theory—it comes from having lived the experience.

QUESTIONS FOR REFLECTION AND DISCUSSION

1. What are some ways you can build an alliance with like-minded Muslims in your community or, if you have children, in the schools?

2. What are some examples of ways you might make a difference in the life of a young Muslim family in your area who may be homesick or feeling isolated?

3. What did you learn about a Muslim's view of illness and death? What are some ways to sensitively approach a Muslim who is facing a serious illness or has lost a loved one?

relating to Muslims in the workplace

The most benevolent, generous person in the world seeks his own happiness in doing good to others, because he places his happiness in their good.

—JONATHAN EDWARDS,
CHARITY AND ITS FRUITS

Merdahd could have been the poster child for American-Iranian relations. Thanks to a scholarship from the Iranian government, which was on good terms with our government at the time, he immigrated to the United States in the 1960s and enrolled in a college in Southern California to study aeronautical engineering. He worked several part-time jobs, lived very simply, worked hard at his studies, and made his dreams come true. He married a California blonde, moved into a nicely furnished apartment in Compton, and had his first child, a baby girl. He was on his way to a lucrative, exciting career in the airline business. Things couldn't have looked better.

Upon graduating, he got a job with American Airlines, which led to an even better job in executive management at Iran Air. Before long he found himself overseeing five hundred personnel, including one hundred Americans. Acting as a liaison between Boeing and Iran Air, he oversaw the purchase of American-manufactured aircraft worth $500 million. With his American wife and three young children in tow, he traveled the world, living interchangeably in the United States and Iran. He climbed the corporate ladder to prestige and financial success. Life really could not have been better for a man of his time.

Without a Country or a Job

Then in 1979, the Iranian Revolution struck, catching an entire nation by surprise as religious fervor spread throughout Iran. Even Merdahd, the contented and loyal American immigrant, questioned his Shah's role in causing the uprising and felt stirrings of support for the revolt. *Perhaps the changes ushered in by the clerics will prove to be better for my homeland*, he told himself. *Perhaps the clerics understand the Iranian people better and will help Iran be a more just and civil society.*

The clerics did take over, some say brutally, not only in the spheres of government and military leadership but at the highest levels at Iran Air, where Merdahd worked. So Merdahd did what he considered to be the most prudent. He salvaged his assets, packed his bags, and fled back to the United States, where his American wife and children awaited his safe arrival.

Merdahd became a man without a country. A man without a job. Like most international professionals who flee to the U.S. for refuge, Merdahd found it more difficult to get another job than he could ever have imagined.

"You're over-qualified."

"You're too old."

"Your English is not perfect enough."

"You just don't fit in."

Rejection resonated through each interview. He could see it on the faces of the interviewers, and he could sense it in their demeanor. His skill set was no longer valued in the United States the way it had been back in Iran. He would need to start over.

His ego still smarting, Merdahd decided to buy a small business rather than take a low-level management job at Boeing. A friend talked him into a dry-cleaning business, which at the time seemed as if it would be easy enough to handle. But the business proved to be a disappointment and didn't generate enough income to support two families. Finances became tight, so Merdahd tried other business ventures, which all collapsed, leaving him nearly penniless.

Despairing and losing self-confidence, he applied for simple blue-collar jobs: a TV cable salesman, a U-haul agent. He finally went back to the industry he knew so well, aviation, but this time as an aircraft mechanic.

But he hardly earned enough to pay his bills and he had problems on the job. Repeatedly Merdahd felt he was being discriminated against and was being treated unjustly by coworkers who lacked his experience. Even his supervisors, he said later, acted as though they felt threatened by his previous expertise and background in the industry.

> Repeatedly Merdahd felt he was being discriminated against and was being treated unjustly by coworkers who lacked his experience.

Finally, Merdahd felt hopeless, an unwanted member of our American society. Something had to change. *It's time to return home to Iran,* he told himself. Living under the new Islamic regime couldn't be any worse than the desperation of being unemployable in the West.

Making a Difference at Work

Does the story of Merdahd remind you of a coworker at your place of employment or someone in your neighborhood who is struggling with insecurity or loneliness or even discrimination? Hundreds and thousands of Muslims have moved to the West with dreams of building a new life. And large numbers have been disappointed because of the difficulty of fitting into our American culture. According to a report from Islam Online news agency, "Since September 11 incidents of discrimination and violence against Arab Americans have sky rocketed. . . . An FBI report confirmed that [in the year following 9-11] attacks against Muslims increased by 1700% over the previous [year]."[1] Many Muslims who had hoped to find financial success and a greater measure of freedom in the West have found heartache, discrimination, and loneliness. According to Ibrahim Hooper, a member of the Council on American-Islamic Relations, "Our biggest obstacle had been ignorance on the part of employers—not prejudice."[2] Americans are ignorant of Muslim values, customs, and religious holidays and are unaware of how to relate to a Muslim in a manner that the Muslim considers respectful.

Many American Muslims who were capable professionals—doctors, teachers, military generals, or engineers—in their own countries, now find it difficult to get appropriate employment in the Western workplace. Unemployed or underemployed Muslims in our midst need our help. Their skill sets are all different. The circumstances are varied. Some are overqualified. Some are unable to perfect their language skills. Some are disheartened and homesick. And some simply do not know how to navigate our job-finding circuit.

> Many American Muslims who were capable professionals—doctors, teachers, military generals, or engineers—in their own countries, now find it difficult to get appropriate employment in the Western workplace.

As Christians we have an opportunity not only to help such individuals find regular employment but also to create a work environment that is both a positive and satisfying experience for everyone. Perhaps you know a Muslim colleague who you sense is struggling with discrimination or uneasiness in his work relationships. You can make a difference by helping to shape a work atmosphere that fosters mutual respect and understanding.

How? By following some simple advice. Consider a conversation I had with a friend from church.

Beth is a vice president of a company in Southern California. She is single and unsure about how to relate to Muslim colleagues, especially those who are part of her staff. "How do I behave around Muslim men?" she asked. "I know their customs are different back home. How do I show respect and still maintain clear lines of authority?"

I was happy that she asked. So little is known in this country about relating to Muslims in the workplace. I gave Beth some simple suggestions that can foster mutual respect and help to avoid hurt feelings.

At the office, for example, women should dress modestly when they work closely with Muslim men. Avoid sleeveless shirts and short skirts or clothing that draws attention to your figure. Don't be too physical. Muslims refrain from hugging or touching people who aren't family members.

"And what about Muslim women?" Beth asked.

"Try not to look down on a Muslim woman who wears a head scarf. Rather, gently inquire about her spiritual life and the choice she has made to cover herself even though she lives in the West."

"Anything else?" she asked.

"Be polite and respectfully acknowledge your Muslim coworkers. It's important to them that you take the time to say 'Good morning' when you arrive at the office and 'Good night' at the end of the day. A woman should try to avoid going to lunch or on a business trip alone with an outwardly religious Muslim man. He may think you're romantically interested in him. And be sensitive to the fact that some Muslims go to the mosque to pray on Fridays."

Beth also wanted to know how American men in her office should relate to their Muslim coworkers. "How could I help them avoid misunderstandings?"

"It's important for American men to initiate a friendship with Muslims in the workplace, knowing they often feel left out," I explained. "It's okay for a man to greet a Muslim man with a warm handshake or a pat on the back. That's not okay for a Muslim woman. Muslims avoid physical contact with the opposite sex. A man should not touch, have long eye contact with, or spend time alone with outwardly religious Muslim women."

My final bit of advice involved a Muslim's different sense of time. Muslims prefer to do business over a leisurely lunch. Americans need to allow extra time. If necessary, clear the calendar for the rest of the day so there's no need to rush off.

You may be asking yourself, "Why should I make all the effort? Shouldn't these immigrants who need to adapt to life in the West work a little harder to fit in?"

Imagine changing places with an immigrant who is struggling to learn the language and find his or her way around in this foreign environment. Imagine how you would feel if a coworker or a neighbor reached out to you and offered some friendship and advice. Relating to Muslims in the workplace offers countless opportunities for acts of

> It's not out of obligation that we should reach out to Muslims but in friendship.

kindness. It's not out of obligation that we should reach out to Muslims but in friendship. We have the right and the power afforded to us by Jesus Christ to be the most benevolent and generous people in the world, who seek not our own happiness but place our happiness in doing good to others.

People of Influence

For every struggling Merdahd, there are thousands of confident, successful American Muslims who have made their dreams a reality and become people of influence in our country. With restless determination they have created for themselves a satisfying home life and have found fulfillment in their careers. I think of my uncle Ahmed, one of the founders and the head anesthesiologist of a prominent hospital in Delaware; my aunt Mastaneh, a senior petroleum geologist who worked on the North Slope in Alaska's Prudhoe Bay; my cousins Setareh, Bahar, and Negar, who are all doctors in Los Angeles; and my cousins Ali and Fasol, who are successful international airline captains. They all pass on their drive and work ethic to their children, who are taking positions of leadership in our society in the medical field, in technology and education, and in politics.

Muslim immigrants do not need our pity in the workplace. They are looking for the same things we all want—camaraderie, respect, and equality. The apparent barriers of an accent, different attire, or dark skin shouldn't make us shy away from our Muslim colleagues. Behind the unfamiliar facade is very likely a capable, intelligent, loyal employee—and a potential friend.

QUESTIONS FOR REFLECTION AND DISCUSSION

1. What are some examples of how a Christian can befriend a Muslim in the workplace?

2. How can Christians be sensitive to Muslims by the way they dress or conduct themselves?

3. Are you aware of discrimination toward Muslims where you work? If so, how can you address it in a gentle manner? Can you think of any passages of Scripture that address this?

4. How do you think the average American feels about adjusting to Muslims in the workplace? Rather than expecting Muslims to adjust to all of our Western customs, how can we meet them halfway?

befriending Muslims on campus

Profound social changes often trace their origins not to sinister conspiracies but to paneled libraries of genial philosophers or the study alcoves of the British Museum or the crowded cafes of universities.

—CHUCK COLSON, *AGAINST THE NIGHT*

The university can be a thrilling environment for sharing ideas which challenge our worldviews, an environment that enables us to engage in open, even zealous, discourse about the things we hold to be most true. Whether it's a discussion of music, art, philosophy, world politics, sexuality, or religion, universities create, for the most part, a safe place for students to shape their beliefs in a way that will carry them for a lifetime. As a college student both in the United States and abroad (in the former Soviet Union in 1986 and in Istanbul, Turkey, in 1988), I revelled in passionate dialogue at smoky Seattle cafés, in front of the Hermitage in St. Petersburg, and along the banks of the Bosphorus in Turkey. Like most college students who wear their feelings on their sleeve, I tried to figure out why the world was so complex and why some people saw the world so differently than I did.

I wanted to make a difference. A revolutionary at heart, I took Eastern European and international studies classes in addition to my literature course work. I felt passionate about my faith and wanted others to know what I had learned. I saw the strategic value of networking with university students to help shape our world and spur one another on as future leaders. I believed in myself and the power of an emerging generation. Cognizant of the fact that the students with whom I came in contact could very well be the next Pulitzer Prize winners, Olympic medal winners, heads of relief organizations, supreme court justices, CEOs of Fortune 500 companies, or presidents of nations, I decided to devote my life to working with university students. Even today, in my thirties and as a mother of three, I delight in my contacts with college students, their zeal for life and ideas, their potential to impact the world for good, their openness to a life of faith, and their quest for truth.

A Woman, a Leader, and a Muslim

In 1988, Benazir Bhutto became the first Muslim woman to head the government of a Muslim country. Her father, Zulfikar Ali Bhutto, the prime minister of Pakistan, sent her to the United States to study at Radcliffe College and to England to study at Oxford University. Ali Bhutto trusted his daughter to study in the West and adjust to the materialistic lifestyle of the West. He admonished her to never forget the huge debt she owed to her country for allowing her to have the means to study abroad. The purpose of her education was for her to one day use it to serve Pakistan to better the lives of others.

> Today half a million international students are studying in the United States. Millions more study in other countries with Christian roots, including England, France, Germany, and Canada. These students are in the emerging generation of world leaders.

Like others who have studied in the West, Benazir Bhutto took her experience as a student in the United States into the highest levels of leadership in her homeland—a Muslim nation. Today half a million international students are studying in the United States. Millions more study in other countries with Christian roots, including England, France,

Germany, and Canada. These students are in the emerging generation of world leaders.

Do you have an opportunity to befriend Muslim students on a nearby campus? In the United States alone, there are nearly eighty thousand students from Muslim areas around the world, representing some forty countries.[1] Many of these Muslims have had little exposure to the positive ideals of democracy, the liberation of women, or to our freedom of speech and worship.

For several years, my husband and I worked as chaplains at the University of Paris. We focused our time mostly at the Cite University, where dozens of dorms were home to several thousand international students from eighty different countries. On any given day, it was not uncommon for me to meet with a student from Algeria for lunch, a student from Kuwait in the afternoon for tea, and a student from China for dinner. In the open atmosphere of collegiate life, we engaged in animated discussions about current events, pop culture, student life, and theology. I delighted in the eclectic environment, which broadened my worldview and deepened my love for Muslims. Over a cup of coffee in a dorm room or sitting on a park bench near a soccer field, I learned about the unique challenges and struggles of international students.

For many Muslim students, it is a shock to leave a close-knit family and community back home and move to the West to study. The freedoms, pace of life, and anti-Muslim sentiment of Westerners is at times overwhelming. For example, Ahmet, a student from Saudi Arabia, finds the transition to life in Boston challeng-

For many Muslim students, it is a shock to leave a close-knit family and community back home and move to the West to study. The freedoms, pace of life, and anti-Muslim sentiment of Westerners is at times overwhelming.

ing. He appreciates the chance to study at MIT (Massachusetts Institute of Technology) but struggles with homesickness, the cold winter climate, and, most of all, the superficiality of relationships on campus. He has a small circle of Muslim friends but resents the fact that his American classmates and the staff on campus treat him with reservation. He feels awkward relating to the women on campus because they behave toward him more like men than the modest women in his home culture. He's tired of his small apartment and cafeteria-style food. He longs for deeper relationships and to feel accepted by his university peers.

"Why do people treat me differently?" Ahmet asks. "I work just as hard as anybody on campus. I try to be polite, do my part, and be a good citizen. But people look at me suspiciously, I can just tell. I'm human too. It's not my fault what happened on 9-11. I didn't condone the violence, and suddenly I feel blacklisted."

Sara, an Indonesian at the University of Southern California, dreamed of making American friends prior to moving to this country two years ago. Enamored with the United States while growing up in an upper-middle-class home with access to American media and entertainment, she is changing her view of life in the West. "Before coming to the United States, I loved the music, films, freedoms, and, I thought, the people. Now I'm not so sure. It's hard to make friends here. Everyone is so busy, into their appearance, and clueless about the rest of the world. I long for friendships where people can talk intelligently about world issues, travel, art, and life outside our little worlds on campus. To be honest," she says, lowering her eyes, "I feel lonely a lot of the time. I don't get to see much of American life other than on TV or the area surrounding my university."

Students at Our Door

In recent years, Christians have shown an interest in reaching out to international students, to mentor them and equip them for leadership. In the foreword to *The World at Your Door*, Billy Graham says, "Over a half million students come from around the globe to study in the United States—right in our own backyard. . . . When these students complete their education and return to their homelands, they assume leadership in international corporations and national institutions. Or they become political leaders, influencing thousands. Unfortunately, during their time in the U.S., over 70 percent of these students never enter an American home or visit a place of worship."[2]

Mark Rentz, from the American Language and Cultural Program, believes that the majority of international students value their time in the West. Rentz has followed the experience of more than three thousand former students who are now leaders in their countries: "When these students were asked about the value of their experience in America, nearly all of the respondents said it was not their academic experience that they remember. Instead, the most valuable experience to them was their time with Americans and the opportunity to experience life in America."[3]

For example, Arafeh, a Palestinian, radiates with gratitude for the chance she has had to study in the West. She moved to Canada eighteen months ago, thanks to the help of an aunt. "I love this country," she says. "My life is totally different here. No threat of war or violence. I can go and come as I please. I'm free to explore my interests and develop my talents." When asked about her faith and how she is treated on campus, she said, "I don't go out of my way to let people know that I'm Muslim, but I figure they usually can tell by my appearance. I hope that they see me as a person first. I want to be seen as a regular student, but I also want to be accepted as a Muslim. It's been very difficult for Muslims around the world lately."

Most Muslim students at our universities are similar to Arafeh. They're deeply grateful for the chance to study in the United States. They long for camaraderie and to forge a successful future for themselves. They're authentic about their identity but want to be accepted on campus just as American students are accepted.

Terror on an Idaho Campus

The lives of Muslim students changed drastically on February 24, 2003, when Sami Omar Al-Hussayen, an admired computer science student at the University of Idaho, was arrested on terrorism-related charges. Al-Hussayen had been trusted and respected as a doctoral student at the university since 1999. Acting on tips, federal agents tapped his phone and intercepted his Internet messages. The investigation culminated in a predawn raid with a hundred agents.

Before September 11, Muslim students at that campus were looked upon as loyal guests. "These people are [now] afraid to email, to talk to strangers, to even leave their apartments," said Liz Brandt, a law professor who counsels students. "We haven't physically put them in internment camps, but we've imprisoned them by fear."[4]

Immediately after Al-Hussayen's arrest, fifteen other students were detained for questioning. "There's fear more of us will be taken," said Mossad, a student. A number of students have left the university, he said, and others are thinking of leaving.

U.S. Attorney General John Ashcroft, in a news conference shortly after the raid, said there had been arrests of terrorist suspects by federal agents in cities all across America.

The majority of young Muslims are dedicated students, working at part-time jobs to pay their bills, turning out for sports, joining fraternities and sororities, and enriching campus life. Many were born in the United States or immigrated to America as young children. They see themselves as Americans or hope to become citizens of our nation someday.

Be a Friend

More than anything, Muslim students need to know you're their genuine friend, that when you spend time together, you aren't taking pity on them and you don't have a selfish agenda. They need to know that you respect them and can separate what you read in the headlines about their identity and faith from them as individuals. Based on my experience in working with international students, let me pass on some suggestions for meeting the needs of Muslim students and building friendships that last:

> The majority of young Muslims are dedicated students, working at part-time jobs to pay their bills, turning out for sports, joining fraternities and sororities, and enriching campus life. Many were born in the United States or immigrated to America as young children. They see themselves as Americans or hope to become citizens of our nation someday.

■ Inquire where their family lives and how often they see their relatives.

■ Acquire a cursory knowledge of their background, the country they are from, and some aspects of their faith.

■ Let your conversation and questions about their culture or faith flow naturally.

■ If they are alone in this country, invite them to your home for the weekend or for the holidays. Be sensitive to the fact that they will feel like an outsider, especially at Christmas and Easter.

■ Be authentic about your faith, but never offend Muslim students by putting down their religion or practices, such as fasting during Ramadan or wearing a head scarf on campus.

■ Respect the fact that devout Muslims prefer to build friendships with members of the same sex and do not date in the same way as Americans do.

■ Invite them to go sightseeing, to a movie or a museum, or to engage in a fun extracurricular activity together.

■ Offer to help them with their transportation needs if they do not own a car. For example, offer to give them a ride to the airport when they are flying home.

■ Invite them for dinner and ask to share a meal from their homeland, either at a restaurant or one you cook together.

■ Suggest the name and phone number of a reliable physician, dentist, hairdresser, mechanic, accountant, or adviser on campus.

■ Invite them to a place of worship and introduce them to your pastor.

■ Remember their birthday with a card and a small gift.

Initiating a friendship with an international student is a wonderful opportunity to invest in the future of the world. This kind of ministry is simple. And it's possible for most people who live near a campus or a bus line. Many colleges are eager to recruit families and individuals who can befriend or house a student for a period of time.

The best place to find out about meeting international students is to contact groups like International Students, Inc. (www.international students.org) or email to information@isionline.org, Bridges International at (www.bridgesinternational.com), or Student Services at a nearby university or college. Staff members generally are friendly and delighted to find volunteers to assist in their work with international students.

QUESTIONS FOR REFLECTION AND DISCUSSION

1. Have you had the chance to visit a campus in the last year or two? If not, what are some ways you could find out about activities open to the public on a nearby campus? Is there an activity you and your family or your small group could attend? Is there a campus coffee shop or bookstore you could visit?

2. How would you feel about being around Muslim students, especially since terrorist attacks have increased in recent years? Have your attitudes changed any? How?

3. Can you think of some ways that you might make contact with Muslim students at a college or university in your area? What kinds of international-student services or ministries are available there?

4. Where do Muslim students hang out on campus? Can you think of some ways you or your small group or your church might initiate contacts with Muslim students?

being authentic about our faith

> It's through our consis-
> tent, holy lifestyle that we
> can show others the way
> to life itself.
>
> —FOUAD ELIAS ACCAD,
> *BUILDING BRIDGES*

Sarah needed a place to stay over spring break. She couldn't return to Iran because of her visa situation, and she couldn't stay in her dorm in Paris because it closed over the holidays. So I invited her to move in with my family for a few weeks.

At the time, my husband and I were working with college students and occupied a small apartment about twenty minutes from the center of Paris. It was customary for us to have students from around the world visit us or stay in our home for a few days at a time. As a new mother accustomed to the action on campus, I loved the company. And Sarah was delighted to have an Iranian-American friend who could sympathize with her situation.

Over those three weeks, we enjoyed spending time together, playing with the baby, running errands, and cooking Iranian meals. One afternoon we spent a few hours painting some old chairs on my balcony, and our conversation turned to spiritual things. I told her about how I had come to faith in Christ after my mother died from cancer.

She was curious why I was not a Muslim like my father. I explained that my father was open-minded about my faith and pleased that I had found direction and meaning for my life. I also explained how he was touched by the number of Christian families who rallied around our family after my mother's death.

It wasn't long before Sarah became bolder and questioned me about the Bible and Christian teachings. She asked me hard questions, becoming more and more animated in her speech and manner. I enjoyed her intensity, knowing she was sincere and not just argumentative. Finally, one day at the grocery store, after another round of rapid-fire questioning about the Bible, I blurted out, "Sarah you'd make a great Protestant because you protest all the time."

"Protestant?" she asked, stunned and suddenly very curious. "What's a Protestant?"

I briefly explained the Reformation and told her about the fiery personalities of Martin Luther and John Calvin. She was intrigued by both the history lesson and by my comparing her to such passionate religious figures. In fact, she liked the idea so much that she wanted to hear more. Over several days, our discussions became more serious. Then one night, the unexpected happened.

The Turning Point

We were home alone, wondering what we could do to entertain ourselves. I wanted Sarah to drive into Paris to meet with some other students even though it was drizzling outdoors. But she was in a particularly solemn mood. She preferred to stay home, she said, where it was quiet and private.

"Come on," I prodded, "it would do you good to get out instead of being cooped up here with a baby and mother." I thought she'd feel better being with other people her age.

"No," she said.

Sarah obviously had something on her mind. She wasn't feeling well. Her mood began to spiral downward and the discussion turned once again to spiritual things.

"I can't pray," Sarah confessed. "I've sinned. My parents are very angry because of some pictures that they saw of me at a nightclub in Sweden."

"Pictures?" I asked. "What kind of pictures?"

"Some embarrassing pictures," Sarah said. "I was with some friends at an Iranian club. We had a great time, and at the end of the evening we took some pictures with a male vocalist. We all huddled together and I put my arm around the singer. The pictures show me touching a man in public. And now the pictures have been passed around and the whole family has seen them. My parents are very ashamed."

I was confused. The event and the pictures sounded harmless. "Surely your parents understand that you were just having fun and that it didn't go any farther than that," I protested.

"Yes, but there are the photos. And I have some relatives who are fundamentalists and are eager to place blame. My parents are angry that there are the photos, not so much that I was out with friends."

"But why can't you pray?" I asked, not seeing the connection. "Isn't this the time to pray when you feel so bad?" It seemed like a natural time to veer the conversation toward the issue of forgiveness.

Sarah looked away, embarrassed. "I can't pray even if I wanted to. It's my time of the month. Muslim women can't pray during their cycle. It's unclean."

"Unclean?" I gasped. "Sarah, God can hear you at any time."

"Really?"

"Yes. He loves you and wants you to feel free to approach him, especially when you feel so unworthy. It's like this." I stood up and walked toward the French doors in my salon. Then I stepped into the entryway and closed the doors behind me. I knocked and waited for Sarah to invite me back into the salon.

"Come in," she said, enjoying the little game.

As I entered the room, I said, "God wants you to invite him to be a part of your life. All you need to do is open the door of your heart."

"It can't be that simple," she shot back.

"It is that simple ... when you approach him with a humble and sincere heart. Jesus can make us clean. Our purity is based on the state of our hearts, not our bodies. He died for us so that we would not have to pay for our own sins. He can make you clean right now."

Finding Spiritual Freedom

Sarah looked down at some Bible passages I had given her to read earlier in the evening. She began to read them silently to herself. She was mesmerized, not taking her eyes off the words. Several minutes passed and then she looked back up at me and said, "I did it. I prayed for Jesus to save me."

"You did what? You prayed what prayer?" I asked in utter amazement, knowing most Muslims spend years coming to the saving knowledge of Christ.

"I asked Jesus to save me," she said again, as if it were the most natural thing in the world. "I want to be forgiven . . . and if Jesus can help me, then I accept his offer."

"Incredible!" I said, still not believing my ears.

There I was sitting in my apartment in Paris, with my eighteen-month-old baby asleep in his crib and my husband out for the night with some student friends, and Sarah had just asked Jesus to forgive her sins. She looked relieved, satisfied with her decision. Little did we know how her life and mine would change after that evening. We had forged a friendship that would weather many storms ahead. At first her family strongly opposed her faith in Christ. Much heartache and many tears awaited us, but Sarah knew she had a Savior who would willingly listen to her prayers and intervene on her behalf . . . regardless of the time of the month it was for her.

> Many Muslims long for committed friendships with godly, moral people they can trust and with whom they can share life's experiences.

Friendship Is the Key

Sarah's story is one of many I could tell that show how eager Muslims are for genuine friendship and how open they are about their spiritual lives. Many Muslims long for committed friendships with godly, moral people they can trust and with whom they can share life's experiences. Whether it's help with learning English, advice on the job, babysitting, or sharing an impromptu meal together, Muslims, like most people, want to feel they belong and are respected and accepted regardless of their different religious background. Don't worry about becoming a cultural expert before you initiate a friendship with a Muslim and express to them your love for Christ. They'll be delighted with the slightest sign of interest, your desire to be helpful.

Opening the Door to Spiritual Exploration

The apostle Paul wrote, "We loved you so much that we were delighted to share with you not only the gospel of God but our lives as well, because you had become so dear to us" (1 Thess. 2:8). Muslims appreciate when Christians are authentic about their faith. So how do we live out our faith as Christians in an authentic but nonoffensive manner with Muslims without wounding their sense of identity? How do we preserve the relationship?

- Be a friend first, taking your time to get to know the Muslims.

- Ask God to direct your conversations.

- Learn about Islam and its view of Christ.

- Offer to pray for your Muslim friend when appropriate, such as when a child becomes ill, a husband loses his job, or a marriage is in trouble.

- Respect their customs, being careful that your attire doesn't offend.

- Be sensitive. Avoid parading or advertising your religious beliefs with stickers, posters, knickknacks, and jewelry, which many Muslims find sacrilegious or offensive.

- Share passages from the Bible, specifically the Gospels, that speak to your Muslim friend's circumstances. Show how Jesus acted toward his followers.

- Share stories, poems, proverbs.

- Invite them to your home for Christmas or Easter.

- Give them a gift: a Bible in their own language, worship music, a book of prayers.

- Visit the sick and those in mourning.

- Handle your Bible with care. Don't set it on the floor or near your feet, which is a sign of disrespect.

- Limit deep spiritual discussions to men with men, and women with women.

- Never argue about or speak of their religion in derogatory terms.

- Listen attentively, seeking to understand their worldview.

Jesus at the Louvre

A few years ago, my father married an Iranian woman and they came to visit my family while we still lived in Paris. Fresh from Iran, my new stepmother had little exposure to Western life. Enthusiastic to share the riches of Parisian life, I offered to take her to the Louvre. Walking the halls of some of the world's largest galleries, we came across several gigantic paintings depicting stories from the Bible. Suddenly my step-mother looked up and said, "Oh, is that Jesus and one of his wives?"

My mouth fell open in amazement. Didn't she know better? Then, as if speaking to a child, I said, as gently as I could, "No, Jesus never married." I explained that Jesus befriended many women, just as the paint-ing showed him with the woman at the well. My stepmother was enamored, and I could tell by the glimmer of curiosity in her eyes that I had an open door to bring up the subject at a later time.

Back home later that afternoon, I made tea, served it on a tray, and asked my stepmother to sit with me on the living room couch. I showed her that I had two Bibles, one in English and one in Persian. I offered to read to her the account of Jesus and the Samaritan woman at the well. She was delighted and agreed. We sipped our tea and conversed freely about Jesus' friendship with women and the liberation he offered them from sickness, fear, and, most important, from their sin. And then I offered to pray for her, prayers for refreshment as well as for less stress and worry in her life.

We had connected. In just three days we had not only become friends but had traversed a spiritual barrier few Christians and Muslims ever have the mutual joy of experiencing. When Christians now approach me about the best way to share their love for Christ with Muslims, I often share this story. I explain how to discern openness on the part of Muslim friends through their eye contact and body language, as well as by their questions and tone of voice. I explain how to graciously point them to Jesus in a way that is relevant to their life experience and level of spiritual interest by first sharing how Christ makes a difference in my life. Some Muslims are simply going to be more open than others, just as some secular Westerners are more open to the gospel than others. As you cultivate a discerning heart, you will know how to approach Muslims and to what extent you can share your faith in Christ. Depending on God's will, with some we only scatter a few seeds. With others we reap a harvest. What a glorious privilege to do his will.

A Few Final Words

I have written this book with a sense of great respect for my Muslim family members and friends. My vision at the same time has been to help my Christian family members and friends gain a better appreciation for and understanding of Muslims living in the West so that they can feel more able and comfortable to befriend them.

I've broached many topics, especially theological differences, lightly and briefly. Some not at all. I've intentionally chosen to write a book that focuses on the commonalities between Muslims and Christians rather than one that focuses on the differences that divide us. Books which draw clear lines of division are necessary to read at certain points in our spiritual exploration. But that has not been my intention nor the way I've been led in this endeavor. My sincere desire is to not offend or anger Muslims, Christians, or Jews, but to share an insider's point of view of the Muslim culture with grace, humility, and love. I will have accomplished a good part of my purpose if readers open the door of their hearts to Muslims in their neighborhoods, colleges, and workplaces in order that these Muslims may come to see the goodness of God and give him thanks. It is not out of obligation but our right to do good and find our happiness in the happiness of others. May your Muslim neighbors "next door" call you blessed and find their hearts warming toward Christ.

QUESTIONS FOR REFLECTION AND DISCUSSION

1. How can you express an authentic faith in Christ without offending your Muslim friends?

2. How can you lovingly explore issues of faith with a Muslim without arguing? How far is too far?

3. How could you pray for your Muslim friends? Can you trust God for the results?

10/40 Window. The area of the Eastern Hemisphere between the latitudes of 10 degrees and 40 degrees with two-thirds of the world's population, which is primarily Muslim.

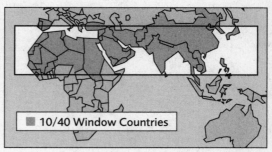

10/40 Window Countries

burqa or **chador**. Veil used by Muslim women to cover their whole body and face.

hajj. The pilgrimage to Mecca required by Islamic law; one of the five pillars of Islam.

imam. Muslim cleric who leads in prayer in the mosque and religious services such as weddings and funerals.

Islam. The word means "submission to God."

Issa. Name for Jesus used in the Koran.

jihad. Religious war or struggle against evil, whether against people or nations who are not under Islamic rule.

Koran (Qu'ran). The final and complete inspired word of God according to Islam transmitted to Muhammad by the angel Gabriel, now perhaps the most recited and memorized book in the world.

Mecca. The holy city in Saudi Arabia which is the place of Muhammad's birth.

Persia and **Persian**. Persia is the former name for the country of Iran. The language spoken in Iran is Persian.

Ramadan. The Islamic month of fasting from daybreak to nightfall; the ninth month in the Islamic calendar.

salam. Greeting of peace.

salat. Muslim ritual prayer recited five times a day.

Shari'a. The Islamic body of law found within the Koran and the Hadith (Islamic traditions).

Shi'ites. Major Islamic sect that follows the teachings of Muhammad's son-in-law Ali and his descendants.

Suffis. Mystical sect of Islam that renounces the world and sees God in all things.

Sunni. An orthodox division of Islam, which constitutes 90 percent of the followers of Islam.

sura (surat). Term used to designate one of the 114 chapters in the Koran.

Western World. The countries of Europe, Australia, and North America.

INTRODUCTION

1. Lorraine Ali, "We Love This Country," *Newsweek* (April 7, 2003), 50.
2. "Muslims Phobic No More," *Christianity Today* (December 9, 2002), 28.
3. Salam Al-Marayati, "Why Muslim Americans Need to Vote," *Islamic Horizons* (January–February 1420/2000), 35.
4. Ibid.
5. "Religion," *2000 Britannica Book of the Year* (Chicago; Encyclopedia Britannica, 2000).
6. Wendy Murray Zoba, "Islam, USA," *Christianity Today* (April 3, 2000), 40.
7. *30 Days of Muslim Prayer and Fasting* (Colorado Springs, Colo.: World Christian News and Books, 2003).
8. Haddad, "National News," *Islamic Horizons* (November–December 1420/1999), 12, 14.
9. Howard Fienburg and Iain Murray, *Christian Science Monitor*, online, November 29, 2001.
10. James Dretke, "The Growth of Islam in the United States," unpublished article (2000).
11. Zoba, "Islam, USA" 48; "N.J. First to Enforce Halal Laws," *Islamic Horizons* (January–February 1420/2000), 37.
12. Abdul Malik Mujahid, "Muslims in America: Profile," www.SoundsVison.com (2001).
13. Zoba, "Islam, USA," 42.
14. George W. Bush, remarks at the Islamic Center of Washington, D.C., Office of International Information Programs, U.S. Department of State (September 2001).

CHAPTER 1. ACROSS THE STREET AND NEXT DOOR

1. Mohamed A. Najmi, "Secular Muslims Find Much to Fear," *Los Angeles Times* (February 9, 2003), B19.

CHAPTER 2. MUSLIMS AND CHRISTIANS HAVE NOTHING IN COMMON SPIRITUALLY

1. Associated Press, "Islam Stand Brings Rebuke," *Los Angeles Times*, May 10, 2003, B16.
2. Kundan Massey, *Tide of the Supernatural* (San Bernardino, Calif.: Here's Life, 1980), 107.

CHAPTER 3. ALL MUSLIMS ARE ARAB

1. Abdul Malik Mujahid, "Muslims in America: Profile," www.allied-media.com (June 6, 2003).
2. Phil Parshall, *Beyond the Mosque* (Grand Rapids: Baker, 1985), 91.
3. Desmond Stewart, *The Arab World* (New York: Time-Life Books, 1942).
4. Parshall, *Beyond the Mosque*, 102.
5. CIA Factbook, 2002.
6. Ibid.
7. "Novelist Nicholas Blincoe on Christianity in Palestine," www.Martin online.com (May 11, 2002).
8. Azhar Abu Ali and Carol A. Reisen, "Gender Role Identity among Adolescent Muslim Girls Living in the U.S.," *Current Psychology*, 18:185–89.
9. Sarwar Sharif and Yasmin Nighat, "Becoming Muslim and Woman: the Bifurcation of Self and Critical Multiculturalism," Ph.D. thesis, Miami University, Oxford (1996).

CHAPTER 4. ALL MUSLIMS HATE THE WEST

1. Kenneth Cragg, *The Call of the Minaret* (Nigeria: Daystar, 1985), 179.
2. Edward Mortimer, *Faith and Power: The Politics of Islam* (New York: Vintage, 1982), 80.
3. Ibid.
4. Ibid., 84.
5. Dilip Hiro, *The Essential Middle East: A Comprehensive Guide* (New York: Carroll and Graf, 2003), 32.
6. Louis Bahajat Hamada, *Understanding the Arab World* (Nashville: Nelson, 1990), 178.
7. Ibid., 182.
8. Ibid.
9. Harry St. John B. Philby, *Sa'udi Arabia*, quoted in Mortimer, *Faith and Power*, 3.

10. Albert Hourani, *A History of the Arab Peoples* (Boston: Belknap, 1990), 9.

11. Ibid., 381.

12. Philip Yancey, "Going It Alone," *Christianity Today* (July 2003), 72.

13. Based on a personal conversation with David Phillips.

14. Milton Viorst, "Why Democracy Is Rejected," *Los Angeles Times* (May 25, 2003).

CHAPTER 5. WOMEN ARE OPPRESSED BY ISLAM

1. Miriam Adeney, *Daughters of Islam* (Downers Grove, Ill.: InterVarsity Press, 2002), 115.

CHAPTER 6. ALL MUSLIMS ARE RADICAL FUNDAMENTALISTS

1. Edward Mortimer, *Faith and Power: The Politics of Islam* (New York: Vintage, 1982), 405.

2. Mary R. Habeck, *Islamists and September 11*, unfinished manuscript.

CHAPTER 8. FORGING ALLIANCES THROUGH OUR FAMILIES

1. Sahar El-Shafie, "Raising Muslim Children in the Public Schools: What Parents Need to Know," *Noor Magazine* (Fall 1998).

2. Ibid.

CHAPTER 9. RELATING TO MUSLIMS IN THE WORKPLACE

1. News Agency in Doho, Qatar, www.IslamOnline.net (January 1, 2003).

2. Salina Khan, "Employers Adjust to Muslim Customs," *USA Today* (April 15, 2003), www.jannah.org/articles/usatodayemployers.html.

CHAPTER 10. BEFRIENDING MUSLIMS ON CAMPUS

1. Tom Phillips et al., *The World at Your Door*, (Minneapolis: Bethany House, 1997), 133.

2. Billy Graham, foreword to *World at Your Door*, by Phillips et al., 13.

3. Phillips et al., *World at Your Door*, 26.

4. Thomas Alex Tizon, "Where Fear, Suspicion Trade Glances," *Los Angeles Times* (April 2003), A24.

Shirin Taber comes from a multicultural background, with an Iranian father and an American mother. She was born in Long Beach, California, and has lived for extended periods of time in Iran, France, and Turkey. Fluent in English, French, and Persian, she brings a unique international worldview to her writing projects.

She earned a bachelor of arts in literature at the University of Washington and pursued graduate studies at Denver Seminary. For eight years, she worked as a university chaplain in the Middle East and Europe. She and her husband, Clyde, are involved in international media projects, specializing in the Damah Film Festival, which explores spiritual experience in film (www.Damah.com).